ALEX'S EYES

A True Story of Hidden Roots

BY
KAY CARROLL

Copyright Kay Carroll 2018 ISBN-13:978-1723499555 ISBN-10: 1723499552

First Edition

To mom, whose love lives on… and whose
sweet memory continues to guide me.

TABLE OF CONTENTS

PREFACE

My great-grandfather died alone. Strangers laid him to rest. That was a century ago. All my great-grandmother knew was that he vanished. When I was a little girl, my mother's memories and the stories that her mother told her about him, were handed down to me. Over the years, I did the same with my children and grandchildren. I wanted them to know Alex and Molly. And I proudly share the last chapter of their lives with you. The triumphant and harrowing life that they led during the late 19th century and turn of the 20th century was not just family lore. They made history, and because of their commitment to family and the fight for justice and equity, I am. I share their lives and the photos and historical documents interspersed in the book to help to tell a poignant tale—the truth of their struggle as American Indians and of a country that relegated them to the margins of its history. One thing my mother remembered, was what her mother told her about Alex: "He went to Washington, D.C. to fight for Indian rights and never came back."

Did fate will it so?

I shared their story with my U.S. History class one afternoon. An observant student peered at a copy of Alex's photograph that I displayed on a side cabinet door, then exclaimed to the class and her teacher, "You have his eyes!"

Introduction

As a part of the Milcreek Pond Series, the books *Milcreek Pond* and *Indigo Sky* are partly based on actual people; however, most details, names, and events are fictional. This final book in the series, *Alex's Eyes*, transitions to actual names, letters, records, events (slightly different years), and struggles created around the documented lives of the real Powell family.

PART 1

1

PAST INTO THE PRESENT

THE MISSISSIPPI DELTA, also called the Yazoo-Mississippi Delta in the 19th century, is the distinctive northwest section of the U.S. state of Mississippi (and small portions of Arkansas and Louisiana) which lies between the Mississippi and Yazoo Rivers. The region has been called "The Most Southern Place on Earth"[1] ("Southern" in the sense of "characteristic of its region, the American South"), because of its unique racial, cultural, and economic history. It is 200 miles long and 87 miles across at its widest point, encompassing circa 4,415,000 acres, or, some 7,000 square miles of loose unconsolidated soil forming a floodplain. Originally covered in hardwood forest across the bottomlands, it was developed as the richest cotton-growing area in the nation before the American Civil War. The area attracted numerous speculators who developed land along the riverfronts for cotton plantations.

As the riverfront areas were developed first and railroads

were slow to be constructed, most of the bottomlands in the Delta were undeveloped, even after the Civil War. Adjacent to the Delta, on land just to the north, was the house where Molly Elizabeth was born.

Molly couldn't remember why her Ma gave her a different name at birth. Having received the sacred name of Mary as a babe, Molly couldn't recall anyone, including her own Ma, calling her by it. She had guessed that after having lived with her for a few years, her Ma figured a name like Molly stuck to her much better. She'd always spelled it M-o-l-l-y, but others wrote down M-o-l-l-i-e—whichever was fine. She wasn't particular about that. M-o-l-l-y was the spelling she'd put at the top of all of her papers since her rambunctious days in Mr. Temple's class–*Molly Elizabeth*. No one ever questioned whatever name she wrote down. Molly thought… that was a long time ago.

"Molly, I can't even get close to you in that dress," her exasperated husband pointed out, as he slid in between her and the chest of drawers.

She ignored the protests of the man pressed against her. "Stop looking out that window!" He said, clutching at her shoulders. "And why'd you make this blouse with these loose sleeves that show off your shoulders? She pretended not to hear him.

"And what's with all these bits and pieces of twine and ribbon tied in bows, ruffles and lace?" he said, twisting a piece of material between his thumb and index finger.

"That's how it's supposed to be made with these decorations," she said, pulling away from his meddling touch. "Anyway, one little ole' dress never stopped you!"

"Sho' nuff," he laughed, pulling her tight and pinning her back against the chest to prove her right.

As husband and wife, most days either started out or ended

like this. Molly and Alex were a well-matched pair. Things between them hadn't changed much since the day the love doused duo found their way back to each other a year ago.

⤜

It had turned unusually cold that late September evening. As temperatures suddenly dropped, Grenada's bountiful, leafy crops of corn, soybean, cotton and rice were swiftly covered with quilts and blankets. It was all that farmers could do to keep their cash crops sheltered from the frost—and alive. But as quickly as that cold snap came, it gave way to a sunny autumn morning.

It was a fitting day for Molly's return. Things were much as they were when she left home for Boston. Her first stop was the rambling estate where she had lived most of her first eighteen years of life.

Shady groves of welcoming pine, pecan trees and towering willow-oak trees still surrounded the near perfect oasis. Molly lived with her mother, the woman she called "Ma," whom she had no intention of again leaving to fend for herself, like she had before.

Before long, there was a freshly designed addition to their own house, crafted by Molly's brother Jake who recently returned from Memphis. He was leaving Grenada again shortly, to marry the women he met while in Memphis. He planned to settle with her and her boy in a town just north of Tennessee.

Molly realized she had gone-on about moving, even after hearing that things would be changing for the better in the South for people like her. There would be new federal laws to make things right and fair. The 1875 Civil Rights Act had passed just six years earlier, making it illegal to discriminate based on race, but it had little to do with life here, at least so far. Lately, there had been reports of more attacks against enterprising men like Jake. Although Molly's family feared the backlash of progress, she thought it even worse if laws that could protect them had never been passed. It would mean returning to the days of no possibility of recourse when people like her suffered indignities.

Jake said the racial violence of the day reminded him of the nightmares that terrorized him when he fled to Memphis and feared for his life. He told Ma and Molly bits and pieces of his story when they were safe together at home. Outside, heavy rains pounded against the pitched roof, as Jake opened up to Ma and Molly how he believed white men's greed had something to do with his father's death or disappearance. He stopped short, though, when he saw the pain that clouded the faces of his mother and sister and shifted the conversation. He focused instead on trying to convince them to move further north and live with him and his new family.

Ma once had plans to leave the South. She abandoned them when her son and daughter went away almost two years ago.

"Folks always looking to the outside for a better life. Sometimes all that matters is what's on the inside of them," she told them. "It doesn't matter, all that much, if they go somewhere else or not."

Further thwarting her brother's plans to keep the family united, Molly told Jake that even she wanted to stay *put* for a while. That's because she hoped to *start-up* a future with Alex.

"Perhaps, one day Ma will decide to leave the South if Alex and I leave," Molly told Jake. She wanted to give him hope that they'd all be together again.

Molly fought the urge to use words like *mayhap,* the language of the South, instead of her usual *perhaps.* But when she thought about it, there was nothing wrong with talking one way or the other. Since she came back home, it was easier to use words she'd previously detested. Molly thought how Ma and Jake would really have a reason to worry if she reverted completely.

"What are you laughing about?" Ma wanted to know. "Oh, nothing," Molly said. "Just happy we're all together, at least for the time being."

As the afternoon approached, the downpour had become

a drizzle. And before long, the sun was peeking through the front window.

Despite what she told her brother about staying put, Molly had little hope that she and Alex, her self-proclaimed intended, would again be courting. Molly and Alex hadn't seen each other since that terrible autumn when the house where she worked caught fire and everyone in the town of Grenada believed that she caused it. That was about two years ago. Molly hadn't been back to that impressive estate since she'd returned. Ma still worked there. She told Molly that the mistress of the house still wore the same sour look on her face. Molly remembered it well.

⋞

Molly had been back in Grenada less than six months, but it didn't take her long to grow restless in the small town where the days crawled. After the parties, people and places she experienced in Boston, Molly had to get reacquainted with the old life that she left behind. Now 18, she was still not officially spoken for.

But this was the day that Molly decided to go in search of the man whose face stayed in her mind. Straightaway, she swept past lakeside willows and crunched pecans underfoot, in search of his towering figure.

There he was. Alex had finally returned from helping kinfolk in Virginia. He was chopping and stacking wood in his father's front yard. His sleek, outstretched arms wielded a long black axe.

After she got close, Molly changed course and tried to retreat. But she couldn't keep from turning back to gaze at Alex as his body heaved and contracted with each swing. That is *my* man, Molly told herself. At that moment, Alex looked taller, broader and more handsome than she'd remembered. His dark, wavy hair, now damp with sweat, clung to his neck. He kept it combed back and off to the side, revealing steely grey eyes and a strong, chiseled jaw. She yearned to hear Alex's voice.

Would he still be interested in me, Molly wondered?

Determined not to find out, she again tried to hustle away without Alex noticing. But as he stood up to wipe his face with a rag, he spotted her as she tried to duck behind the woodshed on the side yard.

When she emerged, Alex wouldn't look directly at her, then his sparkling eyes met her gaze. Older now, with that same gleam she'd remembered, Alex walked over and took Molly's hand. Their locked limbs swung in unison until they moved back near the shed under the wide, shady oak tree. The moment reminded them of those early months together. Molly was unsure of his interest, but that didn't stop her from noticing that her beau had improved in so many ways. The sight of Alex's wide, toothy smile brought back memories of how they first got together. He was the only boy, then, who wasn't scared to come courting.

"You've changed!" Molly blurted out. Alex thought the same of her. He made a point of telling Molly that she'd come back different from Boston.

Molly wanted to tell him that his own change in appearance surely was a not a problem. She imagined what it would be like to place her moist hands on both sides of his shoulders and measure just how much he'd filled out while she was away. The very thought made her blush and excited. So Molly did what was ladylike—she simply held his hand and listened. Then it hit her… Alex's greatest transformation! When he'd first opened his mouth to speak, she hadn't paid attention, having been focused on his near perfect form and everything else.

But this other change. "How did this happen?" She asked. "It's only when I want to," he told her.

"Only when he wanted to?" Molly's mind shouted to a nonexistent audience. Still, she couldn't believe it. Alex was talking proper! Molly remembered a time when he insisted that this manner of "speaking" was uppity and that he only put up with it in her case because he liked her. If that hadn't been enough for their first encounter since getting back, there was one more

thing she found out about him—besides the way he looked and spoke.

"There wasn't any change at all, you were just uninformed," he said, poking fun at her.

"Uninformed? Well, it sounds like you have a different name than the one I was *informed* of," she winced. The sound of a word like *uninformed* coming from his lips was more than she could stand. It left her astonished rather than upset at where their first encounter was now headed.

"Not that anyone ever uses last names much, but I distinctly remember that Jake had mentioned that your last name was *Powton*," she added.

"But that wasn't right," Alex said. "It has always been *Powell.*"

It made no difference to Molly—who had no problem blaming her brother for telling her that convoluted last name belonged to her intended.

"Well, you should have mentioned this before," she told Alex, still a bit stung by his attitude.

"Did any talk about our last names ever come up? I don't believe it did."

Molly's mouth gaped open, not only at his manner of speech, but at how his flippant attitude stepped on her feelings. She turned away and called goodbye over her shoulder. If he didn't care that she'd been thinking of him by some other name, then neither did she.

She always knew Alex's Pa was Choctaw; so, she never did understand why his son would speak with *yes-m's* and *naw's* to the point where she always wanted to correct him. It probably irritated her more because she'd perfected "proper talking" herself, thanks to Ma. Her mother said that it didn't matter how everyone else talked, but that her own "ma" taught her to talk proper-like, and she would teach Molly and her brother to do the same. She said the proper talk would help Molly, especially if she decided to be a teacher. Long ago, she had decided not to let Alex's way of talking bother her, since it was obvious to her and everyone who knew her that she adored him, despite their most recent encounter.

Molly remembered when Ma first began teaching her and Jake proper diction and everything else the determined woman wanted them to learn. Ma was resilient and attractive. She was also finally recovering from her only son being missing for close to two years. He was back, but you could tell she still has a worried, faraway look in her eyes. Picturing her, Molly dreaded the moment when Jake had to break it to their mother that he was again leaving Grenada. He was married now. Jake needed to get as far away as possible from Grenada, Hardeman County, Tennessee and even Memphis for the sake of his new wife. He thought life wouldn't get much better anytime soon with the Jim Crow laws being passed, bringing an end to Reconstruction, and reversing any gains made under the federal civil rights law of 1875. Jake said he had to protect his new family from the things he thought happened to Pa. Her brother thought he realized what happened to Pa. For years, those memories were repressed, but they came flooding back while Jake was hiding out in Memphis. He had left home to travel North for a better life, but ended up a hunted man when he'd innocently befriended a man on the train who was being hunted for robbery. After being mistaken for an accomplice and injured, Jake recovered, and spent two years in hiding under an assumed name.

On that day, Jake unpacked the bits and pieces from his dreams, shared them with Molly and Ma, until Ma ordered him to stop.

"Enough!" she'd said, ending his story in mid-sentence. "However painful my dreams are, Ma," he tried to reassure her, "they led me back to you and Molly."

Ma threw her arms around her son's neck and wept. "I know that your Pa was with you in Memphis. I know the Lord was surely there, too."

Molly recalled other secrets Jake revealed to her before fate had deemed it necessary to separate their family two years earlier.

"*Such is life,*" she'd told herself, when he first left to go North, and cried for more than a week.

At the time, she had no idea why Jake was thinking about leaving them. Weren't they all staying together? Jake didn't have to go. She told him that moving up North wouldn't make him a man, if that's what he was seeking. He was already one. Jake was the only one who shared with her what he could remember of their father. "Can't tell you much, though, seeing that our Pa had to leave in a hurry and never came back," Jake conceded.

"I think he was sad about it though," Jake recalled. "And I was just a baby when Pa left." The few times Molly tried to bring up the subject with Ma, it always turned to other "more important things."

Yes, Jake was the only one who would share some of those secrets with her. Those things hidden, that she still didn't understand why—couldn't be spoken of.

Molly recalled the one that he told her when he thought she was old enough to understand. Ma, then, wasn't aware that Molly knew, and still questions why everyone can't know.

Jake began, "You know our Pa? Well, you couldn't remember him too well, but you know, I do. And, well, he was really, really white-looking."

Jake stopped for a moment to clear his throat, tugging at his collar.

"His mother was a slave, and he had a white man for a father," Jake blurted out.

Molly remembered Jake saying that Pa was almost white. He would say he was caramel colored like Ma and that I got Pa's coloring. She had always thought that was just something for Jake to say only to make talk.

"But that's not all, Molly," Jake said, unraveling more. "Our Pa's father was a relation of Mr. Neuman."

At the time, Molly told Jake she didn't believe him, but he went on to explain how Mr. Neuman's oldest brother had come to America a long time before Mr. Neuman. His views of what was right and wrong were very different than Mr.

Newman's. Jake told me that several years after Mr. Neuman came to Grenada County, Mississippi he found out about his brother's child, who was about 25 years old at the time. He brought him here to work and live on the place, then signed papers to make him free. That's when Ma came here to work. They met, got married and then they had us. That was when Molly learned that Pa was related to Mr. Neuman's brother and a slave woman.

Molly hadn't forgotten when Jake told her about that, even with so much that had happened in her life since then. Jake leaving home and being presumed dead, her going to Boston and Ma breaking down. When Jake came to her with the information he had about his father's identity they both believed she and Jake's Pa were one and the same. Never in a thousand years would Molly have guessed that her father was not only different from Jake's, but owner of the estate on which she lived, the person she most respected next to Ma—Mr. Newman.

It made Molly beyond pleased.

I think I always felt a connection. I was ecstatic when I found out.

Mr. Neuman was good to everyone, especially to us. Now I knew why.

The news had no real effect on Molly's life, to the point where she would almost forget about the connection until many years later.

Even with that, Molly could handle the past, but for the present, it was hard to accept that her brother was going North again. This time he had a family of his own and would likely be leaving his mother and sister for good.

Her eyes glazed over, so much so, that beneath her lids, she clearly envisioned her life as she believed it could have been—enchanted. Molly allowed herself to be captivated by her thoughts, before a *thump, thump* outside sent her eyelids flying wide open to find Alex approaching her front door.

Forgetting their row yesterday, Molly was so grateful that he had come back from Virginia that she'd grasp at any chance to be with him. She remembered the moment they'd all parted ways almost two years ago. Alex stopped by the house on that balmy November afternoon to say goodbye and promised to wait for her.

And now, here he was. As Molly took in his lean, sturdy frame she thought to herself, *he's perfect.*

Aside from Molly's joy at seeing Alex, she wondered why she'd come back South, even though it was with hope that life would be better, especially with the Civil Rights Act of 1875 in place to protect her family. However, in the post-Reconstruction South, men like her brother and Alex were being lynched for any reason. Many of these horrible acts were captured through revolting photographs which were sold to white men and women as entertainment—in print on post-cards, newspapers and event mementos. Photographers would sell their pictures for fifty cents apiece. Even though some whites and full-blooded Indians were sometimes lynched, the images that excited whites most were of black people. In these perilous times, her Alex, so tall, lean, and impressive, had just turned 21. She'd focused mainly on his physical appeal yesterday, when they last saw one another, so Molly could only stare at him when he opened his mouth to speak again—*he sounded so different!*

Noting her incredulous expression, this time he beamed that wide, mesmerizing smile of his at her.

"You know with your eyes and mouth stretched that way, something might fly in," Alex chuckled.

She pressed her lips together and tried to think of something to say, but no words came.

Then he quipped in that familiar dialect she remembered.

"You sho' make a body feel like yo' looking right through 'em or you rightly been a patient all yo' born days." Then *he* just stared.

Molly giggled nervously, not so much because of the *way*

he spoke, but at how Alex's gaze moved down, up, back down and then up to her face again. Molly was well aware that he noticed just how much her figure had changed for the better.

Their purposeful glances at one another moved Alex to break the silence with talk of their early days of courting. Alex remembered taking pleasure in Molly's expression–her delicate oval face, her wide-set, almond-shaped hazel eyes, upturned nose, and Cupid's bow lips. She was even lovelier now than before, he thought.

Molly put her hands up to her cheeks, feeling flush, from Alex's forward, surveying glances. To distract him, she blurted out, "You're different!" at the same moment he began to talk.

Startled, Alex paused, before he began again. "As I told you before, so are you, Molly!"

Alex stepped closer and reached out for her hand. This time, he looked only into her eyes and told her all the things she longed to hear. Not only were her cheeks still burning, but her whole body was set afire. At this moment, Molly knew she was ready to be courted all over again, this time by this new Alex.

That same year, Molly and Alex were married outside, on a drizzly, October afternoon. They stood in a familiar place— among groves of pine and towering willow-oak trees, near the lake on the edge of the town where she grew up.

The first year they were married, Alex and Molly lived with Alex's mother before moving back to Grenada. They would later settle into a place of their own.

Before then, Molly lived with her Ma and sibling in a familiar little house on a country estate, where the owner, Mr. Neuman, also knew Alex's father. He owned a small piece of land that bordered their land and another parcel further south. Many had assumed that Alex's people were sharecroppers, but Alex and his father lived together on their own property until his father died of influenza. But just before the couple married, Alex told his wife-to-be the truth about how his father really died several years earlier. Alex's Ma had sworn him to secrecy. "Pa was murdered in town one Friday night." Alex revealed. "I was at home tending to the livestock."

He gave no details. Alex said the acreage had been his Pa's and his grandfather's before him, since the days when their people possessed all the land in Grenada—when counties were named Choctaw, Carroll, Yalobusha, and Tallahatchie.

2

FIT FOR A NEW LIFE

A UTUMN HAD RETURNED to Milcreek Pond, bringing early evening sunbeams that glistened on the water. On the trees, fall leaves were at their peak and ablaze in red and gold.

Even this quaint, welcoming scene wasn't enough to entice Molly, who was distracted by her Ma's complete turnabout. In light of her earlier reluctance to move North with her brother, Molly's mother, whom everyone called Ma, did move— without any notice, from her small stone- gray, three-room shanty into the owner's magnificent house. She lived in a separate section of the house and from there she was able to perform her usual duties. Once settled in, every week, Ma traveled to visit her daughter and new husband—who had emerged to take their places in the world. With each passing year, Molly watched her mother grow older and then weary, yet she embraced her role in her grandchildren's lives.

❧

Even as the babies continued to come, Molly tried to stay fashionable. She wore her wavy hair loose and had bangs. After a few years, she placed it in a large, tight mass called a bun at the top of her head or off to the side.

The owner's wife, who lived like a recluse these days, continued to stay away from Molly and her family. Molly had befriended the woman's aunt and grew to call her, "Aunt Minnie." It's because of Millicent Grandville that Molly got to live in Boston–the place that became her refuge. Aunt Minnie recently sent Molly a pair of pale green, high-tab-front shoes with a large buckle called the "Cromwell." Molly slipped on the suede, dress boots decorated with lace and metal decals on special occasions only.

Along with the festive footwear, Molly's generous benefactor sent one of latest issues of *Godley's Lady's Book*. Molly thumbed through the pages, relishing the photos of ravishing things she had no use for now that she was back home in Grenada. She was back to being part teacher, and now part farmer's wife and full-time mother, who was too busy to impress anyone with her beauty. Although she still had her long, wavy, chestnut brown hair and 'peaches and cream' complexion, her waist was nowhere near tiny anymore with the baby on its way, and her legs not as lean as they used to be. Her face was also fuller in the cheeks, making her smile just as wide beneath her impish upturned nose.

While in Boston, she'd noticed the women wore non-corseted tea gowns when they were at home. But times were changing. The newest edition of *Jenness Miller* showed women wearing those same tea gowns out on the town. Molly remembered when her shape would have eased beautifully into any one of these new stylish dresses. They would have set off her figure, then an enviable hourglass. The dresses have a narrow waist and flared skirts with bigger bustles that rest on the small of the back. Most ladies she observed in town were attempting to achieve this perfect shape by wearing corsets, full sleeves, and flared, toe-length skirts. One article Molly saw in *Ladies' Home Journal* said that a fashionable evening dress, the way it was made, had the effect of limiting close contact. The new blouses with the "leg-of-mutton" sleeves were worn the most. In the magazine they looked more ornamental than the earlier ones, with bands of ribbon tied in bows, ruffles of lace, and other embellishments following the line of the sleeve across the bodice. Molly noted they looked fuller and much more decorative than the blouses she made or had gotten from Aunt Minnie.

With her belly burgeoning with yet another child, Molly wondered if she should accept any more magazines from Aunt Minnie. She knew she had no more use for most of such beautiful luxuries. And she wondered if seeing them might cause her to yearn for life in the North.

"*No chance of that,*" she told herself.

Molly felt fulfilled in every way. She was in love with Alex, her two children and the one on the way. She looked over as he walked into the bedroom and questioned the array lying across the bed.

"You see how it follows the line of the sleeve across the bodice." Molly explained, pointing to the magazine cover. "Wasn't it nice of Aunt Minnie to send me all this material and another pattern to make it?"

"For what? You're busting out of this one!" Alex teased. "You can't wear it now."

"I know that, but maybe after the baby. I don't know.

"It's pretty though, isn't it?"

3

SURVIVING THE SOUTH

A S A FAMILY, they were resilient, but living as mulattos in the South put that to the test every day. Being part Black and Indian, put Molly and Alex, in a difficult position–especially after Reconstruction ended and people of color lost considerable rights they'd only recently gained after the War Between the States, later referred to as the Civil War. Reconstruction existed during the years after slavery between 1866 and 1880; when the federal government ruled that people of color had the legal right to participate and serve in public office, own land, and pursue a good life for their families.

After Reconstruction, there were only two kinds of people: Whites and Others (including Negros, mulattos, and Indians). The dominant white society often refused to acknowledge any distinction among identifiable non-whites and lumped Negros and Indians in the "Other" category. Thus, in the eyes of the South: Indians, non-Indians (Black/White mix), and Indian mix (Indian/White/Black) were in a similar class as Negros. All were considered inferior groups and were to be segregated from Whites. This practice denied the distinct cultures, histories, and rights of Native Indian ancestry and even led many to attempt to distance themselves from those who were mixed with Black or Negro blood, which some deemed made them lesser.

Starting in the 1830s a great number of Native American Indians were pushed further west of the Mississippi. By the 1880s, many southern whites strongly held the position that all Indians had already *voluntarily* left the South and relocated to a place for them in Oklahoma. Therefore, any still in the South, who claimed to be Indian was perceived as a fraud, perhaps a Negro trying to pass as non-Negro. With this assumption, and with a clear conscious, southerners could dismiss claims from anyone of color who said that they were Indian. Instead, they would sometime choose to assign those persons the label of "Negro" or "Mulatto."

The federal government also reinforced the concepts of race, which had been reported by some of the professed scientific studies of the 18th and 19th centuries. To determine who was Indian, the federal government adopted and promoted the idea of blood quantum: the amount of 'blood' a person possesses from a particular race determined the degree to which that person resembled and behaved like other members of that race.

Blood quantum is based on the idea that race, and therefore behavior, is somehow carried in the blood, and that an Indian who has some European "blood" would be superior to a "full-blooded" Indian. From the viewpoint of the federal government, a person with less than one-half or one-quarter Indian "blood" could be considered non- Indian. And when it came to a white, Indian, and Negro mixture, a single drop of Negro blood made that person a Negro, not Indian or white.

Centuries ago, five Indian tribes, including Alex's father's tribe, the Choctaw, originated in the Southeastern United States and flourished before the arrival of the Europeans. The tribe members were descendants of the Mississippian culture, a civilization built on agriculture and land division. They grew mainly corn and beans, while establishing urban centers and regional chiefdoms with burial and ceremonial structures. Their people were part of complex villages in which the wise elders, kinship and preservation of land meant everything.

Following the U.S. Civil War from 1861-1863, Alex's people, in the Southeast, had to fight to carve out for themselves an identity that retained their Indian culture in a new environment that denied their heritage. In Mississippi, the Choctaw, in particular, refused to be lumped with the Negro community and they constantly sought to assert their separate Indian identity.

4

THE CENSUS MAN

———————

BETWEEN THE CIVIL War and World War II, the United States underwent a profound process of racial reorganization. All branches of the federal government and all levels of governance were involved. The crucial role of the Census Office, who administered the nation's census, was deeply implicated in, and helped to construct its social and political order.

In the United States, race largely defined the social and political order. The American approach to racial classification reflected the particularities of various experiments in racial classification. In any single year and across decades, racial categorization was internally incoherent, inconsistent across groups, and unstable. Mixture between blacks and others was identified, elaborated, and then dropped. Native American Indians were alternately ignored and categorized down to tiny fractions of black and white "blood." These were the times in which Molly and her new husband Alex lived. They learned that not only was the South becoming different, but by these new identification standards, so would the two of them.

᠊ᡃ

Molly had just finished baking cornbread and cooking turnip greens on the woodstove earlier that morning. She welcomed the misty, gray morning that smelled of rain mingled with cooking. It took her back to the first year she and Alex were married...

Falling rust-colored leaves blanketed the front yard, begging to be raked. The tempting aroma of fresh mulberry pie hovered throughout the house–with its steeply pitched roof and barge-board cross gables–and seeped out onto the front porch. Molly's slightly calloused fingers were stained red from the mildly tart, mostly sweet juice. It usually took a few days for the color to wear off. As a girl, she enjoyed sampling the raw fruit from the tree in Ma's front yard; better though was the tasty red ber-ries–plump with juice—as a rich pie filling. When cooked, it dripped with sweetness with an added bit of honey to make syrup for cream custard.

Preparing breakfast, dinner and supper required Molly to start the fire for cooking early and let it burn most of the morn-ing. Alex brought in milk from the dairy cow for drinking, and so Molly could use it to make cream and butter. She usually let the milk sit for an hour. That's how long it took for the cream to rise to the top and separate from the milk. Then Molly placed the cream into a butter churn and beat it until it hardened, first into whipped cream and finally into butter. Once a month she'd use a pestle and mortar to ground up spices like nutmeg, cin-namon, salt and pepper; and store them in glass jars in a cool place out back.

"Good morning again, my one-and-only," she said, snug-gling up to her husband's broad chest. She could feel the rough, coiling hairs against her cheek. But Alex pushed back, reluc-tantly. It was time for him to get dressed and to work. This month's crops needed planting.

Hearing a loud knock at the front door, they moved further apart. It sounded as if someone was in a hurry to get in and get on with their business. It was the dreaded, long forgotten year that the U.S. federal government comes around to take a count of all the people living in this part of the country.

The census enumerators were typically from the village or neighborhood and often knew many of the residents. The U.S. Census Bureau relied on these local people to have some knowledge of most of the town's people, instead of allowing locals to identify themselves on the pages. Although they didn't know everyone, the census enumerator determined racial classification, not the individual.

Prior to 1850, census taking was performed primarily for the purpose of recording tax and land ownership. At the time, most Indians weren't being recorded or included in the *other free persons* or *free persons of color* categories. Beginning in 1850, persons contracted to perform the federal census were encouraged to inquire as to person's self- identification because of the fear of light-skinned Negroes trying to pass themselves off as white or Indian. Given that there were only three available taxable categories; *white, black, or mulatto*; persons who appeared to be mixed- blooded of any kind were to be listed as *mulatto*. Then that person could be taxed and not be listed as any part *Indian* (who were inherently non-taxed).

Molly could barely remember the last time the census man showed up to her house. She was about eight years old when he first came to record her family.

Today, after the man introduced himself and settled in a cane-back chair in the front room, Molly asked him, "Do you want our full given names or just our two names, first and last?"

When the census taker didn't respond, Molly began to just rattle on, trying to be courteous.

Alex's own silence filled the room, causing her to lay her hand on her husband's arm, "Some folks around here want to call him Anthony, but most say Alex—after his pa, Alexander Philips Powell."

Not impressed with the government man's intrusion and lack of respect for his home, Alex didn't feel the need to be too charming when speaking to this not-so-welcome stranger and let Molly do all the talking.

"Next," she told the man, "My given name is Mary Elizabeth, but everyone from the time I was born calls me Molly."

The enumerator wrote down something into the huge black book filled with lines and squares, like the one's Molly's brother used when he kept the books at Mr. Neuman's mill. It reminded her of the pages in his journals she'd found under his bed after he'd disappeared all those years ago.

Molly again touched Alex's arm when she noticed that the man was printing her husband's name as Anthony, instead of Alexander Philips or Alexander or at least Alex P. The man also wrote her name as Mary—which she didn't mind—in place of Molly.

She whispered to her husband next to her, "Why write down the name only *some* folks call you and the name *nobody* calls me?

"Look!" she pointed, before she could stop herself, "He even spelled Powell wrong—with one L!"

Despite Alex's less than gentle nudge to her side, Molly couldn't hold it in any longer before she spoke up. "Sir… the name's we gave you are what folks call us around here—since we were born. But what's that you wrote down? It sure doesn't look like the names we gave you. They call me Molly and my husband by his real name—Alex, but that's not what you've written down on that paper."

Molly pointed to the space number 237 on the cluttered page where the names *Mary and Anthony Powel* had been recorded by the enumerator.

The cheerless man sighed and turned from Molly to stare back at Alex. Tired… his bloodshot eyes took in a mulatto with wavy hair, boot-clad feet and a steady, intense gaze. As the two men exchanged stares without flinching, the opposing sweet, tantalizing scent of fresh mulberry encircled them, and spread throughout the room.

Uncomfortable with this standoff, Molly wished Alex had

tugged at her skirt a lot more forcefully earlier—to get her to keep quiet. Maybe she should offer the gentleman a slice of pie as an appeasement, she thought. She knew Alex believed it did them no good to try and correct those government folks or give them too much information.

Shortly before the enumerator prepared to leave, Alex tried to handle the man's previous, unwelcome scrutiny by whispering to Molly, "From now on… no matter… just go with whatever the man wants to put down," in his over-sized brown ledger.

Alex had no way of knowing it would matter to him one day.

⁘

Such hushed conversation and inquisitive attitudes from people like the Powell's also steered the enumerator to question Molly before he left. With one eye half- shut, and his upper lip curled, he asked, "So, how long you been able to read?"

Standing taller to reaffirm her erect posture, Molly announced, "Not only are we both able to read, but everyone around here knows I am a schoolteacher–since my second year in Mr. Temple's class."

"Uh-hum," the census man nodded, moving his pen slowly inside the lines in the book, then added, "Probably best for you if I mark down you can't."

Molly opened her mouth to protest, but Alex pulled at her elbow—hard this time.

"Mulatto." The man stated, more than asked, and placed an M down in the column next to the name he'd used to identify Alex–Anthony, and another M next to the name Mary on the page near the bottom.

Not to be outdone, Molly blurted, "I first taught myself early on, cause it's not against the law to read and write, and I knew I would need…"

"Age?" The man's voice cut Molly off in mid-sentence.

Choosing to answer, Alex responded, "I'm 21 and my wife turned 18 just this past May."

"Alex, are you sure you are three years older than I am?" Molly asked.

Forgetting the outsider standing in the room, the young bridegroom turned to his bride and held his own private tete 'a tete.

"Now, I'm not exactly sure. My Ma and Pa had nothing written down, but I remember her a few times saying what year I was born, though she could have been off a year or two. I may be closer to your age, you reckon?" He laughed. "Why?"

Molly wasn't sure.

"What does it matter?" He said, solemnly, "My Pa is gone, and as far as Ma and I've counted, I should be around 21 years old now. Are you so sure you are really 18? What month were you born, Molly?"

"Well, my Ma showed me where she put down the day I was born. She wrote it in her old, brown Bible, so I would think it's truthful."

The short stocky man rapped his pen against the edge of the giant ledger and then cleared his throat loudly, before interrupting them.

"So, you a schoolteacher, too?" He asked Alex.

"Yes, sir, I help Molly as much as I can with folk's children she teaches around here, but I plan to become a farmer like my father."

"But my wife here could have gone to one of those teacher's colleges they have for us in Ohio I've read about. "Dear, didn't you visit one of them when you were up North a while back?" He asked his wife.

This was the Alex who used to hate uppity folks? Molly wondered whether Alex was just trying to impress this fellow.

This time it was Alex who felt Molly reach around and then gently pinch his elbow, "Don't offer more information than necessary," she admonished, with a wink.

The census taker frowned at the both of them, shook his head, and then erased what he'd originally put down. "Well,

I'm gonna put you down here as the 'school teacher'," he said, pointing his writing utensil to Alex.

In his rush to finish with "those two mulattos," the census man attacked the page with an inefficient eraser. It left a dark smudge where he'd first written the word "farmer" which was replaced with "school teacher." The smear was several boxes over from Alex's incorrect name of *Anthony*, an error which the enumerator never corrected.

No. 30

sor's Dist. No. 2

tion Dist. No. 64

Note A.—The Census Year begins June 1, 1879, and ends May 31, 1880.

Note B.—All persons will be included in the Enumeration who were living on the 1st day of June, 1880. No others will. Children BORN SINCE June 1, 1880, will be OMITTED. Members of Families who have DIED SINCE June 1, 1880, will be INCLUDED.

Note C.—Questions Nos. 13, 14, 22 and 23 are not to be asked in respect to persons under 10 years of age.

DULE I.—Inhabitants in *Supervisors Dist No 2*, in the County of *Grenada*, State of *Mississippi*, enumerated by me on the 26th day of ---, 1880.

Jno L McElener

		The Name of each Person whose place of abode, on 1st day of June, 1880, was in this family.	Color	Sex	Age	Relationship	Married	Single	Occupation		Health	Nativity		
293 293		Blakely W.P.	W M 32				1		Farmer			Mississippi	N.C.	N.C.
		Blakely Lottie	W F 28			Wife	1		" "			Mississippi	Ga	Ga
312 Kely		Ida	W F 5			Daughter						Mississippi	Mis	Mis
		Blakely	W F 2			Daughter						Mississippi	Mis	
		Taylor Bill	B M 24				1		Laborer			1 1 Mississippi	Mis	Mis
		Taylor Laura	B F 21			Wife	1		" "			1 1 Mississippi	Mis	Mis
2 22		Neal Peter	B M 61						Farmer			1 1 Carolina	S.C.	S.C.
		Neal Caty	B F 40			Wife	1		" "			1 1 Mississippi	Mis	Mis
		Neal Westly	B M 14			son			" "			Mississippi	S.P.	Mis
235 235		Williams Vilet	B F 24				1		Laborer			1 1 Mississippi	Mis	Mis
236 236		Jolly John	B M 25				1		Farmer			Mississippi	N.C.	N.C.
		Jolly Sallie	B F 22			Wife			" "			1 Mississippi	Ga	Ga
		Jolly William	B M 2			son			" "			Mississippi	Mis	Mis
		Jolly Garfield	B M 2m			son			" "			Mississippi	Mis	Mis
237 237		Powel Anthony	M M 24				1					Mississippi	Mis	Mis
		Powel Mary	M F 18			Wife	1		" "			1 1 Mississippi	Mis	Mis

PART II

5

A NEW TIME AND PLACE

AFTER FIVE YEARS of marriage, the young couple already had three children. Molly had little time for anything besides continuous washing, cleaning and nursing babies, but she found a moment to read the newspaper. Both Molly and Alex were more than acquainted with the goings-on in the North, despite living in the Deep South. One Sunday afternoon in July, while reading the *Grenada Sentinel*, she brought to her husband's attention that Ulysses Grant, former president and hero of the War Between the States, was dead at the age of 63. There was an enormous funeral procession for him in New York City. She wondered if Aunt Minnie had been there for that, or the arrival of the Statue of Liberty from France to the New York Harbor, a month earlier.

Molly could just see Aunt Minnie showing up for that, shouting, "This is 1885, liberty for all, you say? Humph!"

∽

As their family grew, a few years later, Molly and Alex settled in a smaller town on the outskirts of Grenada—which was becoming a prosperous community with a population aiming for three thousand. Grenada itself boasted of two-story brick commercial buildings and many new frame residences going up in the business district. By the early 1890s, the town housed over 2,400 people and opened several hotels, including a small one serving blacks. Businesses were springing up all over town. There was a compress company, oil mill, tanning company and a wagon and carriage factory among them. Since cotton was the backbone of the town, there were several licensed cotton buyers and weighers, an industrial cotton shed, and two private ones. For cultural purposes the town offered a collegiate institute, two public schools, one private school, eight churches and an opera house.

The growing industries and healthy economy prompted the opening of the Grenada Bank on Front Street in 1890. It was one of the most successful early banks in Mississippi, which began the first system of branch banking in the state.

By this time, the young couple's family had grown and multiplied. First came a boy, the next year a girl, then one after another with only a year at most in between, which made seven children by the time the next census had rolled around. It was the first to be compiled using the new tabulating machines, the Hollerith electromechanical tabulators—the time required to fully process the counting had dropped from eight years to just six years. This survey year was also notable for the fact almost all the population schedules were destroyed in a fire.

Despite so many improvements all around, conditions for non-whites declined after Reconstruction ended in the South. It had been over 25 years since the Civil War (War Between the States) ended, and the price of cotton had plunged all around the world. They now broke large plantations into small farms for the Freedmen (freed slaves), and poor whites who started growing cotton because they needed the money to pay taxes. Sharecropping became widespread in the South as a response to economic upheaval caused by the end of slavery, during and after Reconstruction. Very poor farmers, both white and black, sharecropped or earned a living from land owned by someone else. The system started with blacks, and when large plantations were subdivided, white farmers also became sharecroppers.

As a girl, Molly recalled landowners, like Mr. Neuman, who provided land, housing, tools, seed, and maybe a mule to their neighbors. They would many times get other food and supplies on credit at Mr. Ole' Mr. Richmond's mercantile. At harvest time, they would share some of their crops with the Neumans, and take some to pay off their debt at the store. There were other farmers who rented only the land, but provided all their own tools, seed and mule. Molly remembered that those neighbors had been called tenant farmers.

In their effort to restore white supremacy, the Democratic controlled state governments of the South passed a new constitution in 1890 that disfranchised all blacks and people of color.. In addition, under racial segregation and Jim Crow laws, states officially included all people of color in the category of "black" and required them to use segregated facilities.

In the midst of these new conditions, Molly and Alex felt the need to settle their family in an inconsequential spot, outside the town of Grenada, but within Grenada County. A place where Alex once lived. It was a small enclave referred to as Misterton, in the north central section of Mississippi, along the Yalobusha River. Their modest but comfortable house and farm were located only a short distance from where Molly grew up outside of the town of Grenada. Surrounding the town were rolling farmlands and woodlands where the Powell family was one of a few non-white landowners. Most everyone got along, and no one had any intention of leaving.

6

CHANGING IDENTITIES

I N THE SPRING of 1892, scores of restless white men, including some in Misterton, searched for ways to stop any man now labeled black—from voting. Years earlier, they had dangled bodies of lifeless men and women from trees, as these white planters tried to control former slaves who had become landowners or sharecroppers. The brutal murders became worse and more frequent at the end of the year, when sharecroppers and tenant farmers tried to settle their accounts. Self-proclaimed vigilantes just grabbed a strong rope and decided to take the law into their own hands.

Molly and Alex both learned about the increased frequency of these acts from the *Colored Citizen* newspaper, which made a point of reporting on the lives of Blacks in the South. The paper stated, *"Any white man who had a strong rope could at any time decide to take the law into their own hands."* The paper also said that those in peril were, "all people of color including Indians, but primarily blacks including those who were once referred to as mulatto."

Things seem to get even more tense, they read, because some voices for equality were passing away, like the inspirational abolitionist writer who as a southern slave escaped up North, Frederick Douglass. The paper wrote, Douglass recently died in Washington, D.C. at the age of 77.

Molly and Alex both feared that without men like Frederick Douglass to stand up for what was right, they would be more vulnerable to discrimination and worse—lynching, as we called them.

There were still some sensible, fearless white men who didn't join in on the organized, widespread hatred of blacks. Like Moncure Conwey, who was once a slave owner and freed all his slaves. Molly wondered why these fair-minded men in many ways are better off material-wise than other whites. She concluded that maybe their success resulted from their so- called goodness. For instance, she'd learned that the fair-minded Mr. Neuman, who began as a corn, soy, and wheat farmer and owned the only grain mill in Grenada County; had become even more prosperous. They published his biography in a book about Mississippi's most famous people. The book said he was "… one of the most progressive, thoroughgoing business men of the same who followed the life of a successful planter and never aspired to publicity. He engaged in farming and also embarked in the sawmill business at Duck Hill, along with his present stand, then in the woods at [Milcreek Pond], and has followed this business ever since, now being the owner of four additional mills: one steam mill near Duck Hill, a water-mill seven miles east of that town, a steam mill at home, and a watermill in Webster County. For eight years, he has operated a good store on his place and does an annual business of about $12,000. He is now the owner of more than 3,000 acres of land in Grenada County, and nearly the same amount of acreage in Montgomery County and in Webster County. And he has a two-acre block and a business block in Duck Hill. They represent all the fruits of his labor since the war. He is now one of the most prosperous planters and business men of the county. He is… public-spirited and has a host of warm friends…."

Yes, times were changing, and despite men like Mr. Neuman, not for the better, as Molly had hoped.

∽

This damp cloudy Monday morning, a knock sounded against the brown wooden door while Alex was outside guiding the mule through the fields. Rather than a horse, the animal better withstood the sultry heat of summer, and his smaller size and hooves were well suited for such crops as cotton, tobacco, and sugar. Alex pulled in the reins of the sturdy beast to slow him to a stop, stepped down, and moved towards the shadowy stranger standing on his wood front porch, with a familiar giant book against his side.

Once inside and seated, the tall lanky man explained the reason for his visit, although no explanation was necessary, noting the oversized black ledger he carried.

However, nearing the end of the century, some categorical details of the census had changed. Now, people who were part Indian or white and looked to have had a black grandparent or great grandparent—were no longer recorded as *mulattos*. The census taker told Molly and Alex that the government was no longer interested in separate categories for *mulattos* or anyone mixed with a drop of Negro blood. Their ambiguous appearance was not to be classified as white or Indian either. However, anyone who was Indian and white–with no visible black descendant—could identify themselves as Indian or white—as they so choose to do.

Alex knew men and women–neighbors—who were especially welcomed into the Indian clan; some said it gave the Indians a feeling of higher self-worth–being valued by the white man and allowed the privilege of accepting him into their fold.

The census man explained further, "Those categories and figures were of little value—*Quadroons, octoroons, and mulattoes.*

They'd already had the change in place long before ex-president (confederate) Jefferson Davis died last year. Anyway, truth be told, we couldn't tell one of you from the other."

As the government had instructed, the man did not record Alex or Molly as *M- mulatto*, which had been removed as a category. The same for their seven children. They, along with their parents, were placed in their newly assigned category, labeled *B- Black*.

7

THE NEW COMMISSION

I T'S MORE THAN a notion trying to keep up with these census takers and what they want." Molly told Alex, once the interloper who'd descended upon their family had left.

Alex put his index finger to his own lips… his signal for Molly to "catch herself," as the man had less than a moment ago stepped outside the door. She'd shared this self-taught strategy with her husband early on, as a way her Ma kept her from "prattling on" when she was a young girl.

However, this time she really had something to say, so she pressed on, "Some want your given name, some want the name folks call you by, some write down your name wrong. I don't see why they keep doing this, if they can't figure out what they want. Ma said they only started coming for *our* information when I just a little tyke."

Once he was sure the census man was a distance away, Alex agreed, "They want to ignore your white father and my Indian one. What's more, what about your Ma and my mother? Where do they belong, 'cause they're mixed?" It never did much for us to have these census people in our house anyway, but it's not of their doing, I suppose. Regardless of what they believe, we must make every one of our parents and grandparents known to our children and their children."

"There was a time," Alex continued, "when all this confusion and separation didn't exist. When people were just people."

"Well, it must have been centuries before either one of us were born," Molly quipped, before hurrying from the room to finish preparing lunch.

It was long time ago… he believed… a time when he didn't even exist, a time that wasn't to return in his lifetime.

"At least I have my own land. They can't take that from me!" He thought. *"They can change what they call me, if they want, but I know who I am, and I have the land my father left me to prove it."*

⁓

Nearing the end of the 19th century, black farmers made up two-thirds of the independent farmers in the Mississippi Delta areas like Grenada County. Alex recalled how the white- dominated state legislature had passed a new state constitution effectively disenfranchising most blacks in the state. He watched helplessly as most newly freed, black landowners lost their lands due to tight credit and political oppression. Most of them had to resort to sharecropping and tenant farming to survive.

Alex realized that these happenings didn't bode well for people like he and Molly who braced themselves for what might happen next.

He recalled the day when he walked the five-mile distance to the only mercantile just outside of Misterton. It was run by a new businessman in town, whom he heard recently had come into enough money to set up shop. Alex and his family always felt as welcome as could be expected in the store. Then one day he was reminded that things were changing.

"What's you say, boy?"

Alex didn't recall ever being addressed as sir by the owner, but he'd never called him boy before, either.

"I'm sorry, sir, I don't understand. I just asked for the usual, a bag of flour, sack of potatoes, and jar of molasses. That's all," Alex said.

"I been meaning to ask you for a while, why you fix yourself to talk like that. You and that gal of yours?"

"Do you mean my wife and I, sir?" Alex corrected him. "You hear me right!" The now irate storekeeper said.

"What's wrong wit' how you fixed them words the first time you com' in here?"

Alex hadn't realized that he'd gotten so comfortable that he dropped the dialect he used the first few times, which was necessary until he knew what to expect in his surroundings. He always had to be on guard lately to protect himself and his family.

The man turned away to wait on the next person in that section.

"And wh'da you wont!" his voice rose at the sight of another man he deemed like the one he'd just spoken to.

"Yes'm, I'z needing to get some meal, yez, suh." The man said, carefully looking away from the store owner's harsh gaze.

The proprietor smiled, speaking to the man cowering in front of him, instead of the Alex waiting on the side. "Now that's what I likes to hear!" He said.

"Now, *he* ain't even here," he added, pointing to Alex, "but *you* can com' on in anytime."

After that day, Alex made it a point to study on people and their ways for much longer before becoming too comfortable with them. And more importantly, never to mention what had happened that afternoon to Molly. That was all he needed, her coming down and making a scene. He knew she would be well within her rights, but he just didn't have the stomach to press for her kind of justice now.

Each day something new was being required of him and his family to survive in the South or elsewhere; it became apparent.

He had heard it told lynching was done these days to protect the virtue and safety of white women, but Alex believed the actions arose out of whites' attempts to maintain control, out of fear that those like him could now possibly share equal rights for land, jobs and social status.

Blacks and most people of color had hoped with the presidential election of William McKinley in 1897, an Ohio veteran of the Civil War, that things might change, but he could not break the "racist stranglehold" of the white South. However, he appointed thirty Negroes to diplomatic and record office positions, along with defying the military by pushing recruitment of Black soldiers. Two quotes Alex would never forget reading from McKinley were:

> *"Nothing can be permanently settled until the right of every citizen to participate equally in our State and National affairs is unalterably fixed. Tariff, finance, civil service, and all other political and party questions should remain open and unsettled until every citizen who has a constitutional right to share in the determination is free to enjoy it."*

Another quote that was seared in Alex's mind was: *"Our black allies must neither be forsaken nor deserted. I weigh my words. This is the great question not only of the present but is the great question of the future; and this question will never be settled until it is settled upon principles of justice, recognizing the sanctity of the Constitution of the United States."*

Despite McKinley's election, not only did atrocities towards blacks pick up, but changes to how other non- whites were being treated came. In 1898 the Curtis Act extended the Dawes Act to the Five Civilized Tribes in Indian Territory, which included the Choctaw. The Dawes Act, passed in 1887, had previously allowed the federal government to break up tribal lands by partitioning them into individual plots.

Faced with an understandable lack of interest [in moving

from their land in Mississippi] by the Five [Civilized] Tribes; the Dawes Commission, originally set up in 1893, received Congressional approval in 1896, to compile rolls of tribe members who would be eligible to receive allotments [in Oklahoma, the newly established Indian Territory]. These allotment negotiations were carried out by the Dawes Commission to the Five Civilized Tribes, chaired by Henry Dawes.

Although the tribes had various census rolls, the Dawes Commission's authority allowed it to add individuals who maintained that it had not included them on the rolls or other lists, making up records of tribal membership. The commission thus undermined the power of the tribes to determine their own membership and, with the Choctaw and Chickasaw, precipitated extensive court action and legal battles over rights to be enrolled.

The process of allotment raised crucial issues both for tribes and for the development of the state of Oklahoma. For the Five Tribes, the tribes determined membership but by the Dawes Commission. The Commission did away with their self-government, including tribal courts. Besides providing for allotment of lands to tribal members, it allowed the Dawes Commission to determine members when registering tribal members, something that was wrought with conflicts of interest. Alex had no idea what impact this one provision would have on his and his own family's destiny.

8

A SEASON FOR SADNESS

WINTER CELEBRATIONS QUICKLY moved in and then out at the start of the New Year. Cold temperatures lingered a while, before ushering in a short warm spring that turned into a long hot summer. During those steamy days and nights of the summer of 1899, Ma passed away at 59. She was resigned to her two efficient rooms behind the Neuman's warm, well-appointed kitchen, with the joy of having her children and grandchildren settled and making their own way.

"She made life wonderful for everyone who knew her." Alex praised his wife's mother.

"Wonderful to everyone but herself." This realization made Molly weep as she held onto her handkerchief and fresh memories of her mother's sacrifices.

"Maybe that's the thing that helped her," he said. "You once told me that maybe everything *you* did in your own life didn't look right to *me* 'cause it wasn't for me to experience. Maybe it was the same for her. Her doing everything for everybody else–well maybe that made her own life meaningful and wonderful–to her. I think you said she called it—her 'joy'."

"I know. Yes, she did." Molly said. "No matter what... she

persevered. She always came through that door [Molly pointed] singing her favorite hymn. Yes, Ma lived as she chose. I can hear singing that hymn she loved. It went like this:

"I love to tell the story, 'twill be my theme in glory, To tell the old, ol story of Jesus and His love."

Molly tried to hold back her tears. Weary, she rested her head on Alex's shoulder. Although the stream of tears was still fresh, she somehow emerged free—as she believed Ma had always been and would forever be.

That night, of all things, Molly recalled the special bond she and her mother shared when she was fourteen. The same event had only a few years earlier been shared with her first-born girl, Eveline [pronounced Evelyn] Francis. It was Molly's turn to pass down the tradition. It was something that united women together but was only discussed in secret. Ma had come to Molly early one morning to show her a small parcel wrapped in a lovely, soft, cotton fabric. She said they were "sanitary napkins," something that Molly would need to use every month. But once Molly married and began to have babies in succession, she hardly ever experienced the monthly ritual which necessitated the use of them.

When her own daughter's time came, Molly was sure Eveline would have more use for them than she had. Although either pregnant or nursing most months, she still remembered enough to tell her daughter how Ma had shown her. Molly wanted her daughter to know everything. She even took Eveline aside and showed her how to use safety pins to keep the sanitary napkins in place, in her underpants. Leaving nothing out, she also showed her daughter how to soak, clean and dry her used pads in the wringer washer. Growing up, Molly had to use the old scrub board. No other such intimate moments would bond a mother and daughter more than this did.

Thoughts like those kept Molly's mind occupied during the most sorrowful time in her almost 38 years on this earth.

She recalled another memory. This one was more worrisome, from many years ago, after she hadn't seen Ma for a while, during those years of being away. She was shocked to see how her mother had changed in that much time. Ma didn't notice the drastic change in her own appearance, but to others, it was obvious. Upon her return from Boston, Molly recalled the tiresome old neighbor who'd picked her up at the train station describing Ma's struggle, and how she'd changed while Molly was away.

This must be how it is when we get older, Molly thought.

We look from our own insides, seeing ourselves change slowly. Our spirit, perhaps? But folks see our outer shell and wonder, "What happened?" Well, I can tell them what happened–it's called living.

Ma mentioned noticing a change, only once, "I don't know why my skin is so dry these days. I must be going back to the dust I came from."

Molly didn't like to hear her mother talk of passing on and steered her to another topic. Once even helping her with a thick ointment to rub onto her hands and feet she was concerned about.

But the time for regrets and reminiscing was past. The moment came for Molly to turn her attention to telling the children, and remain strong for them—not giving in again to the rush of tears that welled up, threatening to seep through all through the day. She pressed her lips together and swallowed hard to hold back the salty liquid that glazed over, and pressed against the corners.

The night before Ma's funeral, she'd need one last time alone–a moment that she didn't want to share with anyone— even Alex. It was then that she opened her top drawer and lifted out her cherished silk, handmade ivory-colored blouse, sent to her from Boston, and made especially for her. The fitted, pleated high collar and cuffs at the end of long puffed satin sleeves, smelled of lilac and jasmine, freshly laundered with perfumed hand soap. It was her most precious possession that would now mean so much more to her because Ma would be wearing it. They would share this final bond from this life into the hereafter—with no one else. Molly's unique knowledge of her own secret sacrifice lit a candle deep within the heart of her sadness. It was that speck of joy her Ma used to talk about. Not even death could extinguish it. Joy was better than happiness. Joy is better.

9

TAKE ME BACK

ALEX AND MOLLY both spent long hours working the rustic parcel he'd inherited from his father. Molly also took care of their growing family. Alex did the bulk of the farming with minimal outside help, besides his wife and oldest children, who were optimistic that the family would be safe and continue to thrive in their new environment.

There were moments when Molly missed her childhood home, the place she'd loved first and best.

In her mind, she could still picture her beloved Milcreek Pond, where… *shimmering waters glistened beyond long branches of tall, swaying willows that shaded the farm on early autumn afternoons. With a life of its own, the lake approached as she and Alex strolled through the avenue of trees, swiveling on their heels to transfix their eyes to the full glorious sight. The tranquil waters held on to various shades of blue, echoing the early morning sky. Near the edge, the color was a light shade, almost opaque; as it moved inward, it changed from a celestial mix to nearly violet.*

Willows and spruces on the other end of the pond were visible on the water's surface. Their leaves rustling in alternating colors, as soft waves undulated, swaying to a song of their own.

Sitting quietly, Molly gave voice to those feelings: "Alex, here and now, we're at a beautiful point on a colorful tapestry."

"We're what, where?"

"It's our moment in time. Our own land, vivid sunshine spreading all across it and us, so warm and inviting. Our children are safe and well fed. Let's just breathe it all in and thank Him for this moment. Who cares what they call us?"

She pressed her hands together. "Baby, let's do all we can to stay this way."

"Of course, we will. Don't talk foolish," Alex said, a bit annoyed that she might be thinking otherwise.

After moving to Misterton, Molly traveled back to Grenada to visit some of the places that she frequented years earlier. Main Street had grown, but Ole' Mr. Richmond's store was still there. His son, who was ten years older than Molly, was now at the helm. Ole' Mr. Richmond himself, whom young-Molly had nicknamed "frog-face," stayed upstairs resting due to his advanced years. But his son still taunted Molly like some old nemesis.

"Well, I'll be dog, if it ain't lil ole Mo.' See yo' still rattlin' on like you used to and didn't make out too good with those shenanigans of yours up North."

Molly ignored him, glad that her husband wasn't there, in case she decided to take the "son of frog-face" down a peg or two. She knew what Alex would say if he were here.

"Now Molly, don't start. You want to set an example for the children to follow."

To which she would reply, *"I am."*

The storekeeper was still saying something to her.

"I see ya din gone an' got yo'self a young'un too," he snorted.

"Yes, and a husband too," she pressed on, with her head held high. "I'm Mrs. Powell now and you better make sure you call me that from now on."

"Humph," he grunted, and then kept quiet. He didn't despise anyone enough, even this gal, that he'd risk losing their business, regardless of the satisfaction he received from taking this one down a peg or two.

When Molly got home, she told Alex what happened. "And he had the gall to ask as I walked out, do I speak that way to everybody. And you know what I told him?"

"What?" Alex asked, though never surprised by anything his wife said.

"I told him, 'No, I don't because none of their actions, or a compilation thereof… ever evoked this kind of emotion in me!'" She then added for her husband's benefit, "Hah!"

"Wow," Alex laughed. "You sounded just like your old self there for a moment."

"I know," she chuckled, "Didn't I? These days, I usually reserve that level of talk for times I'm teaching the children."

PART III

10

NAMES AND LABELS

I N 1900, THE population in the county of Grenada was 14,112. Safely nestled in an obscure corner of the county, Misterton had a population of fifty people-including adults and children. Alex and Molly's family made up almost a quarter of the population of this minuscule little township in the southeastern portion of Grenada County. The place was so inconsequential that it was labeled only as Beat No.2. It was fifteen miles from the main city of Grenada, the county seat—due to its rising commerce and central location on the Yalobusha River. Travelers and salesmen always had to pass through Grenada in the course of their work, so they built a large three-story hotel called "The Chamberlain" near the Illinois Central train station. Molly remembered there had been a time, years earlier when Ma was preparing to move with their family, and she sought weekend work at the hotel to make some extra money.

By the spring, when the next census rolled around, their ever-expanding household included thirteen well-fed, mostly well-behaved, and practical little offspring to help keep the house and homestead running smoothly.

Over the years, Alex studied to become a teacher and a first-rate farmer, like his father. With a houseful of children, Molly kept most of her teaching—that she'd first practiced as a young girl—confined to their home. The lesson's Ma had so faithfully taught she and her brother, along with everything she'd learned from her schoolteacher over 20 years earlier, were being passed down.

Before stepping off of the front porch, Alex paused to look out over the land that belonged to him—a farm of more than fifty lush acres. Twin magnolia trees stood far on the other side the dirt road amidst a grove of pines and oaks. Their glossy leaves turning dark green on top yellowish-beige to rich brown on the underside. Beautiful highly-fragrant splendid little white flowers were emerging on both trees. Its odd-shaped canopy held many large twisting branches that lowered to the ground.

It was another hot spell that had begun a few days earlier with no end in sight. In the afternoon, the children took naps, as a way to cope with the sweltering heat of the sun. They slept during the hottest hours of the day, resumed chores later in the afternoon, and then ate and cleaned inside once the sun has gone down.

After finishing early morning chores in the field, Molly had just gotten them all down, when there was a knock on the back door. Startled by the loud, heavy knocking, she jumped up to answer. Alex had just entered through the front door, as the census man came through the back door, this time around. They were not sure why. As part of his routine questioning, he got around to asking Alex's occupation, to which he proudly stated "farmer." He hated that he'd taken on and still owed amortgage, only because of two terrible years of poor crops. But they were almost done paying that off.

With pride, he squared his shoulders back and watched the enumerator mark down under OWNERSHIP OF HOME, 'O' for Owned instead of 'R' for Rented.

RADE, OR ION	EDUCATION.				OWNERSHIP OF HOME.			
YEARS of age	Attended school (in months).	Can read.	Can write.	Can speak English.	Owned or rented.	Owned free or mortgaged.	Farm or house.	Number of farm schedule.
Months not employed.								
20	21	22	23	24	25	26	27	28
	Yes	Yes	Yes		O	M	H	230

Molly said what Alex was thinking: "It's our land, and it's almost paid off, free and clear." She offered the stranger more information than Alex felt comfortable giving him.

She had no regrets this time around when this other enumerator also refused to put down "school teacher" next to her name. All folks had to do was watch and listen to each one of her busy, calculating little brood to know–whoever took care of them had to be some kind of teacher and a darn good one at that.

TWELFTH CENSUS OF THE UNITED STATES.

SCHEDULE No. 1.—POPULATION.

B

Supervisor's District No. ___ Sheet No. ___
Enumeration District No. ___ 14

State _Mississippi_
County _Grenada_

Township or other division of county ___ Beat No. 2 ___   Name of Institution, X ___

Name of incorporated city, town, or village, within the above-named division, X ___   Ward of city, X ___

Enumerated by me on the _22_ day of June, 1900, _Thomas R. Williamson_, Enumerator.

LOCATION	NAME	RELATIONS	PERSONAL DESCRIPTION	NATIVITY	CITIZENSHIP	OCCUPATION, TRADE, OR PROFESSION	EDUCATION	OWNERSHIP OF HOME

(Handwritten census entries — largely illegible)

	Susan	Wife		Mississippi	Alabama	Alabama			
	Joffie	daughter		Mississippi	Alabama	Mississippi			
	Mattie	daughter		Mississippi	Mississippi	Mississippi			
	Linda				Mississippi	Mississippi			
		Head		Virginia	Virginia	Virginia	farmer		
		daughter		Mississippi	Virginia	Alabama			
		Head		Mississippi	Tennessee	Tennessee	farmer		
		Wife		Mississippi	Alabama	Virginia			
		daughter		Mississippi		Mississippi			
		Head		Mississippi	Mississippi	Mississippi	farmer		
		Wife		Mississippi	Mississippi	Mississippi			
	Mary P	Wife		Mississippi	Mississippi	Alabama			
	Charles H	Son		Mississippi	Mississippi		farm laborer		
	Francis P	daughter		Mississippi	Mississippi	Mississippi	farm laborer		
	Joseph J	Son		Mississippi	Mississippi		farm laborer		
	John E	Son		Mississippi	Mississippi	Mississippi	farm laborer		
		daughter		Mississippi	Mississippi	Mississippi	farm laborer		
		Son		Mississippi	Mississippi	Mississippi	farm laborer		
	Clarence	Son		Mississippi		Mississippi	farm laborer		
				Mississippi	Mississippi	Mississippi			
		Son		Mississippi	Mississippi				
		Son		Mississippi	Mississippi	Mississippi			
	Minnie C	daughter		Mississippi	Mississippi	Mississippi			
	Marshall P	Son		Mississippi	Mississippi	Mississippi			

The familiar giant ledger had been trimmed down a bit, Alex noted, as the census taker put down his name next to number 253 as, *Anthony P.*, like the one before. This time Alex *did* question it, but the man snapped, "It's Anthony that's recorded on the last census ledger and mayhap the one before. Can't change it now."

With that, Alex guessed it would be futile to push to correct it anymore. It did not occur to him that this decision could one day bring his integrity into question.

He looked on as the fellow wrote down the government's acceptable labels concerning himself:

B-Black, M-Male, H-*Head of Household, Born: May 1860.*

Quietly noting how the slim black ceremonial writing instrument slid across the page, Alex recalled how in the last census session, ten years earlier, the man had put down, *M-Mulatto* under the heading, *"Color or race"*.

Alex felt times had changed in how the world viewed people like his family. He knew he was born in Mississippi, along with his father and his mother in Virginia. Either way, he wondered why they never recognized the Indian blood passed down to him by his ancestors.

"Are every one of my grandparents included in the 'Mulatto' or the 'Black' label?" Alex wanted to know.

Alex strode into the kitchen and beckoned for Molly's attention, because once again, he noticed on the next line for number 253, the man had written down *Mary E.* instead of *Molly E.*

Molly followed him from the back of the house to the front where the man stood. This place was a lot larger than the first place they lived, or the one Molly had grown up in.

Before leaving the kitchen, Alex asked her, "Are you still upset about your birth name going down on those government papers? I thought I'd ask since you told me you always go by Molly, not Mary, even long before I'd met you."

"That's fine. I don't mind Mary," she whispered to her husband standing next to her.

By the time she had been a wife and mother for almost

twenty years, Molly had learned to like her Christian name. She didn't believe it before, but it was pretty too, she thought, like in the Bible… Mary. She was a proud mother of these twelve fine-looking children, whose names this census man now asked for. She beamed as he wrote them all down on his page, along with each of their ages, the year and place they were born. Then she thought, "Well, at least he got the children's names right."

Once the official, tiresome fellow was finally done, the couple closed the front door and locked it. Looking out the window at him as he stepped off the porch, Alex still didn't know if having strangers coming into their home was doing them any good. The man said it would, because Alex and his family were now being counted as citizens. But that still didn't give them the same right to vote with the outlandish poll tax and grandfather clause in place.

Alex thought, "*Or a right to speak our minds or get any help from our government when we need it.*"

It had become important that people like Alex—mulattos, blacks, and even poor white sharecroppers' band together and help each other out. The great majority of them were farmers. Among them were four main groups, three of which worked for white landowners: tenant farmers, sharecroppers, and agricultural laborers. Those who owned their own farms were to some degree independent of white economic control. Yet, it didn't seem to matter if the mixed raced, blacks or Indians worked together–even owned land–they still weren't allowed the vote in the South... unlike their sometimes even poorer white neighbors.

In every instance, the poor white neighbors had an advantage, but Alex never faulted them. The way things were going, he believed, it wasn't their doing. He didn't even fault his Indian friends about the treatment he got from their tribal leadership– how they ignored him. His Indian friends and relatives—he fondly thought of his cousin Cioak—were all partly his people. But it did hurt Alex when some of those friends got the fatted calf from the leaders, when Alex could hardly get them to recognize him.

Even before 1896, when the U.S. Supreme Court ruled in favor of Jim Crow laws in *Plessy vs. Ferguson*, upholding "separate but equal" facilities for all people of color, there wasn't much they could do besides be counted in the census. And soon those families began to lose rights to land they'd claimed as their own before and after the Civil War.

Alex regularly prayed that someone would follow the U.S. Constitution and include all folks, even those mixed with black and Indian, to allow prosperity to trickle down to them.

11

LOVED AND LOST

A FTER THE CENSUS man left, Alex settled down in his favorite oversized, brown tweed chair near the front door and pictured their names; his own, his wife's and children, just as the man had written them down on the bottom of the page in his heavy ledger.

Such a l-o-o-n-g list. Alex couldn't help thinking. *How can we keep having children year after year, if I can't take care of them? But I should be ashamed thinking like this… cause we love each one of them, and couldn't do without the older ones help, still maybe we shouldn't have anymore. But when she's a part of you, how can you stay away from the woman you adore? I can't keep from loving her.*

Alex tilted his chair's position, leaning over the armrest to gaze at his once-again pregnant love—how she easily glided to the children's bedrooms to assist them with the daily house-keeping tasks, even now. So cautious lately, she called out to them to wait until later and sit awhile to cool off.

Molly herself plopped down in a chair just outside one of the bedroom doors. She turned and saw her husband half- smiling at her and puckered up at him. After that, she yelled back to each of their busy brood who had yet to obey her command, and they dropped one by one, wherever they were, to rest.

Their mother kept them shaded indoors as much as possible the last two days from the sizzling rays. They drank plenty of water. She watched out for her husband too, warning Alex that even her homemade brew wasn't a good idea for him during the heat wave. It had a healthy touch of liquor in it and would likely make him sweat a lot.

If anyone had to go out in the day, in heat like this, Molly dressed the children in light-colored, loose-fitting wear to cover as much skin as possible. She even made whoever ventured out, including Alex, protect their face and head by wearing a wide-brimmed hat like the one she wore. For as long as they could, everyone avoided strenuous work during the hottest part of the day. If they had to work, everyone took frequent breaks.

The whole family, even the younger ones, knew why Molly was so strict with her regimen. Although unrelated, Molly could never forget the Yellow Fever epidemic of 1878 when so many people in Grenada had passed on. Most victims were buried in the Odd Fellows Cemetery on western edge of the city or in the "Yellow Fever" cemetery east of the railroad. They buried many of the black victims in a now abandoned cemetery north of the Odd Fellows Cemetery. Molly recalled how Ma saved many residents with her concoction of garlic and vinegar. Molly has always been leery of fever and illness since then. But more so, her heightened fear developed many years after that, when she'd lost her precious child because she couldn't recognize the signs of heat exhaustion.

Now–if anyone experienced heavy sweating, pale or flushed skin, even if their forehead felt cool, she would take action. Or if anybody slowed down their movements, like they were going to drop, said their head hurt, or looked as if they would throw up—she put them to bed to doctor on them.

Just two days earlier, she was not sure how it happened, but Alex had to haul in their oldest son, who insisted on getting his work done outside in midday during a heat spell. His breathing was labored, his skin red and hot to touch. Alex helped his son to a bed in the coolest part of the house, shaded by the thick willow-oak tree. Molly gave him water and put a wet towel on the back of his neck and underarms, then his siblings took turns cooling him with ten pleated fans. Molly made sure he didn't close his eyes for long, while they worked on him, no matter what, fearing he would not be able to open them again. She would not let what happened ever happen again—not like before. And everyone knew it. So, they followed her every instruction during these treacherous hot spells.

"He said when he's doing something, like his chores, he just doesn't think about the things he's doing. I used to be like that." Molly said about her headstrong son.

"I was going here and there, doing this and that, being spirited sometimes, or happy... living life my way—and forgetting," she added.

"Forgetting what?" her son asked.

"Ohhh, I forget there's a time limit, a finish point for us. Just like there are so many numbers on a timepiece. It goes 'round twice, and it's the end of one day, then maybe the start of a new one. After sundown, late at night when the moon is the only light, that's one complete rotation, moving towards another starting point or finish line."

"A time limit on us, huh? I think I know what you mean... well, I try not to think about that," he said, pulling up from the bed and removing the tepid cloth from around his neck.

"The older I get, the more I think about it, like my Ma did, I suppose, after she had me and your uncle. I'm praying, even right now, that not another one of my children's time arrives before mine, 'cause I don't believe I could stand it."

He took hold of his mother's arm, his eyes mirroring her relief—now that he was safe. "I'm sorry," he told her.

Molly never talked about the child she'd lost. It's possible she had pushed the memory out of her head. It was too hard to bear and to remember.

12
SILENT SUNSET

A COOL BREEZE CAME through an hour before sunset, bringing the sweet, honey-like scent of magnolias floating through the unshuttered, front windows. While still keeping an eye on her eldest son, Molly ventured out onto the porch to join Alex who had stepped out moments earlier. He helped his expectant wife pull up a stool alongside him and they lingered a while, squinting at the hills saluting the sun, as the day came to a close. Molly rubbed her hands along the apron tied to her thick waist, still wondering about these boundaries being placed upon them. Was it something she should try not to be aware of–not mindful at all?

She could tell from the deep crevice lining the right side of Alex's face that he was worried. More than likely about how he was going to support his family within the limits imposed upon him.

Hoping to help ease his tension, Molly began talking, and talking, and then talking some more.

"Out of breath, huh?" He asked, when she finally stopped.

"Naw, I just gulped in a hunk of air and pressed my lips together tight to stop myself," she said, laughing. "You know I hadn't had to catch my breath like that in a long while... made me think of the times Ma and Jake stopped short of smacking me for 'rattling on too much."

"Who could forget?" Alex said. "But you don't go on so much anymore."

She wanted to say, *"But, I need to, just like that young girl— this anxious woman needs to go on."*

The sun, now hidden behind the hills in the distance, prompted her to stand and stretch before going back inside. She wanted to give her Alex time to be the man he was–alone. She knew there was only so much time.

In her mind, she offered up lovingly...

... we do what we can, 'cause we have life now... all we can do is live it... you, me, and the children... best as we can, my brave, strong husband.

13

SONG OF THE FAMILY

A FTER BEING MARRIED for nearly 20 years, and having marched into a new century, Alex wanted more than anything to secure his position in the world for him and his family. Talk was going around that land owned by any man who wasn't white and who claimed Indian ancestry would have to be secured with the Indian Nation to be retained or replaced. While land owned by anyone else non-white would be taken away without any recompense, if they couldn't prove Indian ancestry. Alex wondered if he would be surprised at anything that came his way after this Dawes Commission was organized several years earlier.

Just yesterday, he had been outside working before the census taker arrived. And now, thinking about all that'd happened in the last year, Alex went into the side drawer of his wooden desk, pulled out a paper tablet, and began to write. He knew what he planned to do if for some reason those land grabbers came for him.

Along with creating his own writings, Alex pulled out some

of the papers he helped his neighbors decipher. Stories had been circulating the last few months about escalating violence in the area. Vigilante groups known as the Red Shirts, the White League, rifle clubs, and one other unnamed club were now working openly; and they were better organized than when they tried to keep their actions secret as the Ku Klux Klan. Some of Alex's neighbors had already experienced violence and terrorism when the Democrats—a political party that wanted the old South restored—first began to rise to power. For years, many of the non-white families had been threatened if they tried to exercise their voting rights under the 15th Amendment, which had been added to the United States Constitution over 30 years ago.

On the day of the 1900 election, the Red Shirts were even more obvious than in 1898. They rode around the voting polls with their guns and horses, intimidating people of color and anyone else who sympathized with their plight.

Alex pounded his fist hard against the desk and put aside the letter he'd been writing.

"Maybe one day this will change, if we can just get somebody to listen," he said.

The year prior, he'd spoke before his neighbors, in one of several secretly held meetings on how much he'd hoped their lives would improve–but would it? Shoving his hat onto the back of his head and forcing it down in front, just above his eyes, Alex trudged out to examine the soil he'd been carefully tending yesterday, before the government man interrupted his daily routine.

As forewarned, not long afterwards, news that hit even closer to home struck the Powell family.

⁂

"What do you make of this?" Molly said, handing over the back page of the *Grenada Sentential*.

Glimpsing the writing before the page reached him, Alex dropped his pipe and snatched the newspaper from Molly's fingers without meaning to. "Let me see that," he said.

He slowly perused the smaller words under the headline and article below.

"You mean I have to petition now, as if my Pa never lived! I have to beg or don't even get to keep my land? MY LAND!"

He couldn't believe those who had no right, could come along and tell him that all he knew–never was. Even more suspicious, Alex could never forget his mother saying that his father was killed in a fight with another man who had wanted to buy their land for almost nothing. Alex knew his father was not one to start a brawl and would try to talk things out with folks. Alex had no idea if this thing with the land had anything to do with it, but he did know that he owned it since his father died, and that's what he told that census man to put down.

Watching the color drain from Alex's face, Molly drew back and hurried to get a cool cloth.

"I've been paying our mortgage to the bank... on time... each and every month... and now white man comes along and says that the land belongs to the government to do with as they please."

Silence blanketed the room for a long while before Molly felt it was safe to pass him the towel and say something she hoped would make things easier.

"It may look that way, but it's a good thing you've gotten nimble with writing and talking your way through things," she said, giving him praise wherever she could find it.

"We-e!?" He shouted. "You know they won't listen to you!"

Molly knew this wasn't her Alex raising his voice at her. She and her man had always worked together.

She and her man had always worked together.

She held her tongue, then remembered something, and shouted to the bedroom, "Sista." Molly's nickname for their oldest daughter, Eveline Francis.

Eveline, who had busied herself with morning chores, whipped two rumpled sheets through the air and smoothed them back down over the beds.

"Don't forget to tuck all the corners underneath this time, tight," her mother instructed.

"I won't, Mother," she yelled back. "I'll also check on the stew and cornbread, when I'm done in here."

Photo of Eveline Francis Powell around 1910 (10 years later).

It was getting close to early afternoon. The boys would soon be called in for the biggest meal of the day, cornbread, potatoes, and ox-tail stew— dinner. Molly held a small portion of the stew over for supper later that evening.

With her crumpled feelings now smoothed out, Molly focused again on her husband, who sat painfully silent.

"Honey, you know whatever I can do to help— I want to. Either way, I promise to be doing most of the worrying," she said, looking down into the half-closed eyes of the newest baby latched onto her breast. This one made number thirteen.

There was always the sound of a baby crying in the Powell house. Their cries were as much a part of the chaos as they were the sweet music of life that filled their days and nights. Without missing a beat, every able-bodied family member contributed to the daily functioning of the Powell household. Alex and the boys spent most of their time outdoors work-ing crops in the fields, feeding and managing the livestock, and sometimes hunting. Molly and girls worked mainly in the house cooking, cleaning, and outside they fed the chickens and smaller livestock.

When it came time to butcher animals, neighbors joined in to share the workload and the reward of meat. A few times they got a bit of beef, like today, but most days it was chicken. Pork was the staple meat; however, they didn't have that all the time, either. Alex recently had acquired a hog for pork, whose taste improved with curing. Before then, he'd traded wheat and corn with neighbors to give his family table some of the savory flavorful meat a few times a week.

Usually in the fall, the neighbors would gather, everyone working together, but also to catch up, sharing news and gossip. What always began as a chore turned into a social event, espe-cially at harvest time. This year a few more families pitched in to help the Powell family bring in their cotton, wheat and corn crops. After the work was done, everyone celebrated by the fire–singing and dancing. Every man was the same then.

But all that changed in the little enclave called Misterton when outsiders intervened to alter its ceremonious peace.

"I've got to do something about this right now! Take a look at this week's paper." Alex urged.

"I've just seen it, dear—remember? But what can *we* do?"

"Nothing else to do but go to see those Dawes Indian rolls and search them to be sure my name's there."

"But you know *both* your parents weren't full Choctaw, like Cioak's were," Molly reminded him.

"Yes, but my Pa was a Choctaw, so my name should be there." Alex used the end of his pipe to stab at the article in the newspaper that had taken over his thoughts.

Molly's mention of Cioak brought back memories of Alex's departed friend and distant relative, whose calm, familiar features clouded his thoughts. They had been close as almost any relation could have been, and it tore Alex apart to remember how his lifelong companion had become so bitter as to die the way he did. There was so much he wished he'd said to make his cousin understand that he didn't have to do the things he did. But it was too late now.

"What if it isn't'? Molly's voice broke in. "What?" Alex asked, startled.

"What if your name isn't on the roll?" Molly spoke methodically.

"Oh," he said. "It'll only be missing because my Ma was part Portuguese and had been a slave. I once heard, though I don't think it's true, that Choctaw go down the line of the mother for inheritance. But Pa was a full Choctaw. I know one of our neighbors, Jim, said his Pa was on it. And his Pa was only half Choctaw and his ma White. So maybe, I'll have a good chance."

"Here," Molly said, handing him the baby and adjusting her light covering over her shoulder. "I'll get you your special paper and writing utensil from the desk drawer."

"Okay, I'll go lay him down." Alex said, returning after getting the baby settled.

"Thank you dear," Molly reached out to caress her anxious husband's freshly, shaven face, then added, "It won't be any problem to keep the children busy outside or in the other rooms, so as not to bother you while you write to someone about those Indian Rolls."

After three days of pen to paper, Alex cleaned up and shaved off several days of stubble, and then rushed to the postmaster to send off his most intelligent, respectful correspondence to date.

The days of waiting began and turned from weeks to months. It was more than either of them could stand, but they made do with each other's support.

"No word yet?" Molly asked, noting her husband's slow, stilted pace when he crept in from his visit to town. She was sure that Alex first stopped at the postmaster.

Alex forced himself to perk up and slipped his arm around the waist of the woman he'd loved since he was 18, and she, almost 15. He recalled the time she sent her brother to meet him at Milcreek Pond in her place. And when he finally knew for sure that she was the one for him. Then, when Alex thought he'd lost Molly that time she went to Boston to escape her life in Grenada. He never wanted to disappoint her, especially now.

"Naw," he answered, smiling at her with a bit of spirit that wasn't in him. "Haven't gotten word from the postmaster to pick up the letter yet, if that's what you were thinking." He didn't tell her he'd stopped in anyway.

Molly spoke cheerfully, trying to ease her man's hidden pain, "It's been only three months, so it won't be long now."

He wrapped her up in his arms, then stroked her soft, wavy, waist-length hair, now sprinkled with tight, graying strands. Alex thanked God that she had come back to him instead of staying up North when she had the chance.

14

TRIP TO MERIDIAN

NOTHER SIX MONTHS passed. It was a warm, muggy evening—still early, but already getting dark outside. Pies sat cooling on the kitchen table.

Sitting in the living room darning, Molly almost jumped from her favorite wing-back chair when Alex burst through the front door.

"Molly, look. I got word from Indian Affairs. The letter was waiting at the Misterton Post Office." Alex waved the long, thin envelope through the mulberry-scented air.

Praying it was good news, Molly was so excited she snatched it from his hand and cried, "Doesn't feel like much of a letter."

"No matter, it's a letter," Alex said as he yanked it back from Molly. They want me to come to testify in front of the Indian Commission on April 4 about my land request. Molly, look. Look at it!"

"Meridian, you have to travel all the way to Meridian?" she shrieked. "That's over a hundred miles from here."

"About 130, I believe," Alex said, after pulling out the state map tucked into the front desk drawer.

Molly sighed and put away the sewing she was halfway

finished with—having let out the hem of two of her long skirts for Eveline and shortened a pair of breeches for the youngest boy.

"Can you get the Illinois Central train from the station in Grenada into Meridian?" She asked.

"I don't believe so. There's no passenger stop there, just a junction. But I can get a wagon train into Meridian. I hear they replaced that old mule-drawn, trolley system with a new electric one. I'll use it to get across town."

"However you get there, it's going to cost us," Molly said. "I know," he agreed.

Molly kept thoroughly re-reading both pages of the letter. "Didn't you send your own letter out almost a year ago, and they're just now getting word to you to travel all the way down to Meridian and testify?" she asked.

Then, she pointed out, at the top of the first page, the name Anthony Powell, as it was listed on the census.

"Mr. Anthony Powell," she repeated. "Not Alex."

"Darn it Molly! If that's what they want to call me, then that's who I'll be!" Alex insisted. "You're not very excited about this letter, I get it, but at least it's something."

"Yes, I still am, but I see now we're going to need a lawyer for sure, and we haven't talked about how we can get the money."

Molly reached around to calm her man, and slide her fingers through his soft, dark wavy hair. At that moment, she knew he was right. At least it was something. Her Alex was one good-looking specimen, Molly thought. It's one of the reasons why they already had so many children and another on the way.

Molly tried to recall how much they paid when they needed a lawyer once before.

"I have to check," Alex said, "But don't you agree a practiced attorney was the way to go, especially after receiving guidance when we prayed about it. Remember we read, "'Plans fail for the lack of counsel, but with many advisers they succeed,' in Proverbs 15:22?"

"So, that's why you wanted more than one lawyer?" she

asked, remembering how, with no money, Alex had tried to hire a law firm.

"Doesn't matter now. Things are looking up for us, Moll, aren't they? I know this is the answer to what we've been praying for since last June. I've got to get my breeches, dress shirt and waistcoat all pressed, or maybe my Sunday suit cleaned just so!"

"Hey, I don't think you ever called me that before," she said.

"What?" Alex asked, not sure what his wife meant.

She kissed him lightly on the lips. "Moll. You said Moll. That's sweet."

Cherishing the gleaming smile on his face, Molly vowed to no longer be a naysayer and only speak to what the future held.

"You're going to look so good. Those men on the Indian Affairs Commission will surely give you your rightful inheritance just because of that!" She proclaimed, throwing her eager arms around Alex's strong neck and holding on tight enough for him to feel it.

~

With everything at stake, Alex chose took a stagecoach instead of wagon train to Meridian the day of his testimony. There would be no possibility of him arriving soaking wet or getting dust covered along the way. Molly brought all the children into the front room where they all joined hands and prayed for her husband and their father— the man with everything depending on this moment—to receive help from above. She ended with Ma's favorite verse, Isaiah: 41:10, "Fear thou not…"

Passing through downtown Grenada on the way, Alex noted the new places for business now constructed on the public square. Grenada was originally formed from the two towns of Pittsburg and Tullahoma which were settled in the mid-1830's. The town was a quiet trading center for many years until the coming of the railroad in 1860. As the junction of two important Mississippi railroads, the location became important as a rail center. Then in 1870, Grenada County was formed, and Grenada was named the county seat. A building boom followed which began in 1880, and now commercial buildings and residences were springing up. It was early morning, and businessmen stood outside in front of their Italian-designed establishments with cast iron storefronts and arched windows, some smoking cigars. Alex passed the Chamberlain Hotel and thought of Molly's dear mother.

Now past Grenada, and on the road to Meridian, Alex passed open meadows, woodlands, and then one-story frame residences with vernacular designs, log cabins, and dilapidated shanties.

As soon as Alex arrived at the courthouse, he was called forward.

Photo of Alex Powell, Approximately 1910 (9 years later)

15

ALEX TESTIFIES BEFORE THE DAWES COMMISSION

Actual Excerpts

[Author narration <u>underlined</u> and in brackets]

DEPARTMENT OF INTERIOR
Meridian Mississippi April 4, 1901

In the matter of the application of *Anthony P. Powell*, for himself and his thirteen minor children, for identification as Mississippi Choctaw. Anthony P. Powell, being first sworn upon his oath, states as follows:

Examination by the Commission

Q: Is your mother living:
She died in 1890.

Q: What was her name?
Fannie Powell

Q: How does it come that your father's name was Wilmer?
> *You see my mother was a slave and he had to take her name because she was a slave.*

Q: Your mother was a colored woman? [Wide-eyed, the questioner looked from Alex to the stenographer.]
> *Yes, sir.*

Q: (She) claim any Indian blood?
> *No, sir just my father.*

Q: So, your mother was a slave, you say?
> *Yes sir.*

Q: What proportion of Choctaw blood do you claim to have?
> *One-half.*

Q: You get your Indian blood from your father?
> *Yes, sir.*

Q: Your parents, did they always live here in Mississippi?
> *Well now, I have heard my mother say that her parents never did live here. She came from old Virginia.*

Q: Her father lived in Mississippi?
> *[Hearing the judge say 'your' father, as he was questioning Alex's parentage, Alex responded, with his own father's origins. Later asking for a copy of his testimony Alex believed the judge did state "Your father", which directly lines up with preceding and following questions. Alex questioned whether the transcriber took information down incorrectly.*
> *1*
> *-I have never know him to live anywhere else.*

Q: It will be necessary that you furnish this Commission with evidence of your marriage to Mollie E. Powell, in connection with the application made by you at this time on behalf of your thirteen minor children. This may be forwarded to the

Commission within a period of thirty days from this date, and it will be filed con considered in connection with this case.

Q: The claim for your children has the same foundation as yours, of course.

> *Yes sir.*

Q: How long have you lived in Mississippi.

> *All my life.*

Q: Born and raised here?

> *Yes, sir in Choctaw County, in this state. And I have never been out of the to live, just visit*

Q: Did either you, your father, or any of your children, ever received any benefits whatever as Choctaw citizens; ever get any money or land?

> *No sir, they never got any money.*

Q: Are your names to be found on the Choctaw Tribal rolls in the Indian Territory?

> *Not that I know of.*

Q: Did you ever make application for yourself, or on behalf of the minor children to the Choctaw tribal authorities in the Indian Territory of citizenship in the Choctaw nation?

> *No, sir.*

Q: Did you make application to this Commission in 1896, for citizenship in the Choctaw Nation?

> *No, sir.*

Q: Did you ever appear before this Commission prior to this time?

> *No, Sir.*

Q: You never have then ever been admitted to citizenship in the Choctaw Nation either by the tribal authorization of the

Choctaw Nation or Congress approved June 10 1896, or by the United States Courts for the Indian Territory on appeal?
 No, sir.

Q: Never was recognized in any manner as a citizen of the Choctaw Nation:
 No, sir.

Q: What do you appear here for at this time:
 To be identified as a Choctaw citizen

Q: Do you claim under any particular treaty between the United States and the Choctaw Nation?
 The Treaty of 1830.
 [Alex thought of Cioak and how his family tried to hold on to a portion of their land under the same treaty. Now, years later, he was trying to do the same.]

Q: When was that treaty made? Do you know? Who made it" Where was it made?
[This judge asked questions of Alex, that he was sure the man knew the answers to. If not, he didn't deserve to sit in that seat, Alex thought.]
 The treaty was made between the United States and Mississippi Choctaw Indians; the reason I say that, I asked how I could prove up my father's, get his portion that was in there and they said that was the only way.

Q: Who told you this?
 My lawyer told me so, and that I had better get up my proof.

Q: Do you claim under any particular article of that treaty?
 Article Fourteen

Q: Did you ever read that article?
 No, sir.

Q: Do you know anything that is contained in it?

Not anymore than I claim under the treaty of 1830, article fourteen: that is what my lawyer told me. I am just telling you the truth.

Q: Do you know whether any of your ancestors ever complied with the provisions of that article of the treaty of 1830?

No, sir. I don't. I don't read and don't know anything about it. If they did. I know nothing about it.

Q: What one of your ancestors was living here in Mississippi in 1830 when that treaty was made?

I suppose my father.

Q: Do you think he was living here then?

I know I found him here.

Q: Do you know if he was ever recognized here at that time as a member of the Choctaw tribe?

Yes, sir, I suppose he was.

Q: You don't know?

No, sir, I just suppose he was; he never was a slave.

Q: You remember your father, do you?

Yes, sir, he was living with me up until his death.

Q: How old were you when he died?

I wasn't quite grown; I am forty-one now; you can judge for yourself.

Q: Did he look like a full blood Choctaw Indian?

Yes, sir.

Q: Did he speak the Choctaw language?

Yes, sir.

Q: Did he move out west with the Indians when they first went out there in the early thirties?

Not that I know of.

Q: Did you ever hear him tell about the Choctaws moving out to this western country, where they live now?

I never did hear him say anything about it at all.

Q: You don't know whether he ever claimed or received any land here in Mississippi, as a beneficiary under the fourteenth article of the treaty of 1830?

No, sir; I know he never did, for I would have gotten hold of some of it; I went to school, and if he had had money, I would have got it.

Q: You think he never got any land at all?

No, sir.

No sir got no money from the government, for he would have spent it.

Q: Is there any additional statement in regard to your case that you want to make at this time?

No, sir

Q: Have you any affidavits, statements or other proper papers you desire to present in support of your claim?

L.P. Hudson Attorney for [the] applicant, here asks permission to provide written evidence in support of this application within thirty days from this date.

Permission is granted.

16
WHAT'S IN A NAME?

B Y THE TIME Alex returned home from giving his deposition, it was near evening and the air was balmy on this spring day.

"Alex, baby you're back," Molly cried. Her outstretched arms welcomed her worn husband and pushed past her swollen belly.

"I have a good feeling," he said, easing into her grasp, "I spoke the way they expected, by adding some touches of the old Alex. You know, that's how they like to hear us speak."

She nodded.

"And baby, they wanted to know everything that anybody ever told me, plus what I knew about my life up 'til today."

Alex was glad to be home. Without notice, he reached for his pregnant wife, hugged her tight and lifted her up off the floor. Still lean and muscular at forty-one, he kissed her long and hard to celebrate the moment. The children looked on, feeling good seeing their mother and father happier than they had in a while.

"Whoa, slow down, baby. Remember we still got the one in here."

"Right, right," Alex said, as he patted her bulging belly.

The next words he blurted out seemed to come out of nowhere.

"Oh yeah, by the way, I told him you were a half-breed." Molly couldn't believe what she heard. "Wha… !? So, did you tell them about my Ma having some Choctaw, too?"

"The examiner didn't ask, and it makes no difference.

They asked about my Ma, who looked almost white, but she was still a slave." Alex said, as he put his boots away in the box by the door.

"So, did they give you anything to show for your long, tiresome day?" Molly wanted to know.

"Nothing but this," Alex said as he reached into his pocket for a long slip of paper. He handed it to his wife.

"That's all they gave you," Molly asked. "I wonder how they got all of our names for this piece of paper. Did you give our names and the children's ages in that letter you sent?"

"I dunno. I don't recall giving them all the children's names," he said, sitting down next to her. "But I did give them my name as Anthony P, since that's what that enumerator put down in the census book last time he came here. I'm confounded as to what name they want. Everyone knows people down here go by two names, and neither has to be their real name, either. Folks start calling them by it and it just sticks."

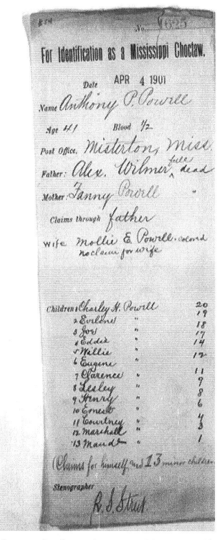

Identification slip for application as Mississippi Choctaws

Molly nodded, then laid her head against his strong shoulder. "Sometimes families forget what their given name ever was," she laughed, "but you know, I heard up North they can get information about folk's birth these days, even those like us. We've forged into the 20th century, and almost anything's possible. If anything, they probably pulled the children's names from that enumerator's book when he came in here to conduct the census this spring."

Alex agreed. "Now, what's to eat?"

Molly eased up from the sofa to warm up a hearty plate of pinto beans, salt pork and cornbread for her husband.

"Did you file for me too?" Molly asked, after he got settled at the table.

"I didn't want to confuse the matter anymore than I had to, especially since the land we're trying to keep once belonged to my father."

"You do know Ma was some part Choctaw? You just said so."

"Yes, I knew, but as I said, this may be hard enough just to get them to do the right thing by me and the children. If we get added, then, I tell you what, we will apply to have you added too. Okay, baby? Oh, now I remember, they didn't give me that slip of paper with the names on it until I left, so they got yours and the children's information from me at the hearing."

Alex stopped talking, then tore into the plate piled with hot food.

Molly sighed, "That's fine, baby. Still, I think it's obvious to anyone with half-an eye to see... that you are Choctaw."

She took a deep breath and allowed her free hand to massage her husband's firm neck. Her other hand cradled her belly. "If there is anything that is good to come out of that Commission, it's that you should be able to keep your land. Your Pa left it to you. Everyone knows you own it."

With his mouth half filled with buttered cornbread, Alex muttered, "It's strange that you say that because after I walked out, I stood in the hall for a second, and heard them saying something about my appearance, that I think they may have written down."

"What'd you hear?"

Wiping his mouth, Alex said, "I recall one of the men

saying, 'He's got half Choctaw blood. Looks somewhat like he could be some with his straight hair and skin coloring.' "

"Hmmm," Molly murmured aloud, then thought, I *don't know how they could think anything else.*

"Want some more pinto beans?" She asked. "No thanks, baby. I'm full. "

Molly and the children didn't bother Alex the rest of the evening, except once.

"What's all the commotion?" he asked, stepping outside his door to see who was pounding against the wall.

"That's our children," Molly apologized. "This is why our neighbors call them the wild, strong-mannerly bunch."

Alex laughed and shook his head, going back into his room to go over every word that was spoken to him, and those from his own lips, in Meridian that day.

17

A VISITOR

<hr>

AFTER GOING OVER his testimony in his mind, Alex had some reservations.

"Molly, I was so nervous. Now, I don't know what I told them. I wasn't sure how I should speak, so I settled on somewhere in between."

"I know you said you didn't speak proper English, the way you finally learned."

"I may have some, I think, but my knowing how-to doesn't mean much here in the Deep South."

"Well, it does to me." Molly insisted.

Alex sat down, grabbed the back of another spindle wood chair, pulled it over, and beckoned for her to sit next to him.

"Molly, sometimes it means *too* much to them. Don't you understand? More than it does to you and me—but in another way." Alex continued, "The last thing I need now is for them to start wondering about me even more than they already act like they are. That's why I think I did right by telling them another thing I didn't mention when I came home," he said.

"What was that?" Molly asked, squirming in her seat now.

"Well, I said that I couldn't read."

"Alex, no you didn't!"

"But it was the truth, really. They wanted to know if I saw some papers my Pa may have had when I was a boy. I said I don't think so, but it didn't matter 'cause I couldn't read."

Molly dropped her hands into her lap and stared at the floor. She didn't say a word.

"Now baby, they didn't just come out and ask me if I could read—at this point in my life. They asked if I read some treaty papers my father had years ago. So, I said I couldn't read."

"Alex, why?"

"What was I supposed to say? I can read now, but couldn't have read anything before I was at least eight. I can't help it if they believe I still can't. That's on them. I think they were trying to make me stumble onto a falsehood or something. Asking me what I know about amendments and treaties and all. Like they even know. I just know my father should have had some papers. What would I be doing knowing what was in them if he did? A boy, I was!"

Alex got up from his seat next to Molly and went for his pipe on the side table in the living room.

Alex had gotten all of his inheritance from his own Pa when he was killed over some minor disagreement by a neighbor who went to prison for it. He had been living with his father on his land up until his death. Molly found out that Alex's parents weren't allowed to marry like she and Alex. His mother had been a slave. She was half- black, white and Indian. The man who enslaved her years before, had to give permission for her to marry. But the law wouldn't put it down on paper as official. Until Alex mentioned it, Molly had never asked about his mother's background. She didn't recall if Alex said they were always together as a family.

When Alex testified in Meridian, he stated his name was Anthony P. Powell. It was already on government papers. He believed it would confuse them, if he offered up the name of Alexander P. Powell. Years before, the enumerator mistakenly put down the name Anthony on the census. She suspected

Alex planned to take his chances and let it be. It was his way of saving what belonged to him. He didn't care about anything now— just saving his family.

"Did you feel the need to make yourself different to those men?" Molly wanted to know.

"I didn't do that, they did, over 20 years ago, when that man came around and wrote down what he wanted to! Maybe he didn't know how to spell. I dunno. It's a good chance he wasn't any better at writing than those little urchins you used to play teacher to down at Milcreek Pond. It wouldn't have mattered if his bosses knew he couldn't spell, which I'm sure they did. He would have still gotten that job as a census taker."

"Don't get off point, Alex, they put you down as Anthony on one and Alex on another. For me, it was Mary on one paper, and Mollie on another. They spelled our names different ways and may blame us now if they find out you can read," Molly said.

"I'm going to use what they did wrong to my advantage," Alex announced, "Take something they did wrong to make it right for us! What other choice do I have? Just this once, Molly, please trust me. I got to do what has to be done to get what we need."

"Anyway, it wouldn't matter to these government people." He continued, "Remember what happened when I did try to get it right in 1890, since I wasn't young and intimidated by the enumerator, like I was when he stormed into our home the first time?"

"Yes, I remember exactly what he said," Molly recited verbatim. "'Too late to fix-it nows. After all, it don't matter 'cause ain't no need to get names right for part-Black Indians, like yo'selves.'"

Alex shuddered when Molly recounted those hateful words, not bothering to mention the enumerator's comments when he tried to get it straight again in this past census.

"Look, honey," Molly said, trying to soften the mood. "Remember when we were first courting, at least when *I* told everyone we were," she laughed, and poked his side. "I was just fourteen and wanted you to talk better. But I wanted you to be Alex, more than I needed you to talk proper."

"Yeah, I knew you wanted me to. Even when you stopped correctin' me, I still knew better. You wanted me to be more like you and your folks."

"Maybe at first, but now that I think back, that's really not so. It never was. Did you ever hear me say anything like that? I loved my handsome, strong, beau anyway I could get him." She purred, then kissed Alex hard on the lips. "I just wanted you more than anything. And that's all I need again. I just need you to be you. No one else."

They held and comforted one another, taking a moment from constant worries and struggles to appreciate their sacred gift of love. It had blossomed like Molly's belly, year after year, as it filled with another one of their beloved offspring. Each child was a way of reminding them of the power of their yearning for one another and the strength and beauty of what their union could produce.

18
MIRROR IMAGE

HISTORY HAS SOMETIMES been a friend, but mostly, it has been the enemy of my people," Alex told his neighbor the next afternoon, after reading that President McKinley had been killed. Alex felt sure it was most likely for what McKinley believed about equality and justice for all men. Yet there was no time to mourn the loss of this good man. Alex's friend Jim had come around to report that two strange men were asking questions about all the neighbors, especially Alex.

"Never seen them 'fore and they had some papers they wanted me to sign too, but I didn't," his friend confided. "Wasn't sure what they was up to or what I was signing."

"I can't say the same for everyone else, man. I saw Mart, down the other way, lettering on something one of those men had sitting on a writing board. He was the same one who told me they was insurance men going around checking on claims."

Alex was grateful for the information.

"I've got to say you're one heck of a fella, Jim, for a white man," he joked. "You're a friend and a neighbor. Your ma and pa both listed as white on their birth record, right? And you say they 'recollect that they can go back to their great-grands from the early 1700's who had some Choctaw blood. That was enough to get your Ma and Pa onto the Indian rolls."

"Sho', they're on it, I am too," Jim said.

Alex grinned and kept his arm around the shoulder of a young man who had, at times, been like a brother.

"Well, I have no problem with that, my friend, it's as it should be," Alex said with sincerity. "But here I am. I know my father was a full-blood Choctaw, and I can prove it. Have affidavits from you and more than a few upstanding citizens, but because I'm not like you, they can't or won't believe me. And they will take my land here and won't replace it in Indian Territory."

Jim told Alex that didn't seem right. "I wish I could be of some more help to you," his friend said, looking down at his boots.

"Thank you, Jim, but it's not your burden," Alex said. He lifted his arm from around his neighbor's shoulder and extended his right hand. "You're a good, fair man, Jim; you and your whole family."

As Jim and Alex returned to their homes in the distance, they looked so much alike, it would have been hard to tell them apart.

19

THE RACE BEGINS

―――――――――――

ALEX HAD BEEN waiting months for a decision after his testimony in Meridian. Unable to wait another day, he sent off an inquiry in January about the status of his application. To avoid any misunderstandings, he had settled upon just using his initials A.P., instead of Alex or Anthony P., in any correspondence to the Indian Affairs Commission. Notifying him that they had yet to make a decision, the *Commissioner in Charge* addressed his response to Alex's inquiry by using the simple initials Alex settled on.

Muskogee, Indian Territory, January 14, 1902.

A. P. Powell,

      Misterton, Mississippi,

Dear Sir:

      Receipt is hereby acknowledged of your letter of the ninth instant, in which you ask to be advised as to the status of your application for identification as a Mississippi Choctaw and as to whether you can hold land in Indian Territory.

      In reply to your letter you are advised that no decision has yet been reached or opinion rendered relative to your rights as a Mississippi Choctaw. When a decision is reached you will be notified of the action taken by the Commission.

      As to whether you can hold lands in the Indian Territory, your attention is called to the following provision of the act of Congress of May 31, 1900:

    "That any Mississippi Choctaw duly identified as such by the United States Commission to the Five Civilized Tribes shall have the right, at any time prior to the approval of the final rolls of the Choctaws and Chickasaws by the Secretary of the Interior, to make settlement within the Choctaw-Chickasaw country, and on proof of the fact of bona fide settlement may be enrolled by the said United States Commission and by the Secretary of the Interior as Choctaws entitled to allotment."

                 Yours truly,

MC 1625   Commissioner in Charge.

Response from the Muskogee Territory Commission January 1904

By this time, any Choctaw who had stayed behind in Mississippi and didn't migrate to Oklahoma were considered third-class citizens—just behind freed slaves. Although, on his mother's side, Alex was a mix of black, Indian and white, he was also raised to not throw away his father's Choctaw heritage. People like him, in the government's view, had few rights than even the blacks with mostly African ancestry, who could better fend for themselves. Alex sensed that people like him were at the bottom of the heap, left with no one to fight for them or their rights.

As nearby Grenada's population of 2,500 slowly doubled in size, the pressure for citizens like Alex and Molly to leave increased. The opening of new industries continued along with the overall commercial health of the community. By 1902, more commercial buildings were springing up downtown, along First Street, Green Street and around the public square and near the train depot.

The next morning, Alex shot up out of the bed, screaming like out of a nightmare. He threw off the covers and frightened Molly, who jumped up and ran towards the children's rooms.

"We can't keep having babies," he kept shouting, "if I can't take care of the one's already here! How can we? If I have no land to work, how can I make a living? Renting some else's land won't leave us with near enough money to live on. Not the way we have been living. What am I going to do, Moll? What? M-Molly, baby, what's gonna happen to us and the children?"

Molly climbed back in the bed, rolled over and sat up on one elbow. She laced her other arm tight around her man's shoulder and looked into his luminous, deep-set gray eyes. Then, she eased Alex back down onto the covers.

"No more children, you say? Whatever happens, you tell me how I can stop loving you with all my might—the man I've always adored?" Molly asked through her tears.

The next morning, Alex's mind turned back to what was giving his head all the trouble—that didn't want to move on.

"I've heard there's a lot of names of folks from these parts on the rolls." He took up the conversation where he'd left off the night before. "I wonder why so few, if any, of the half- black/half-Indians I know are on those original tribal rolls."

"Is that why if they make the mistake and put you down as mainly Indian and Portuguese and don't mention black, you won't correct them?" Molly asked.

"Why should I? When your mother is any part black, even when your father is a full blood Indian, they act like they don't want to record your birth as anything. I had to take my mother's name, but they wouldn't even let me have my Pa's last name, even though they were permitted to marry."

Alex went on a rant.

"Who knows what I am?" He shouted, throwing up his hands, and prompting Molly to hold her finger to her lips to get him to quiet down, and not rile the children today.

"Shhhhh!"

"I just want to be a man," Alex cried out, "Have my wife and children able to live, to eat and have clothes, and a good place to live!"

Alex still spoke forcefully, but quietly now. "So, tell me, who do I have to be for that to happen?" He asked through clenched teeth.

"All I ask is to be treated the same as any Choctaw with mixed heritage–like our neighbor Jim. And at the same time, I don't want to be treated any better *or* worse 'cause my mother was mixed with white and black."

The steadfast duo of Molly and Alex grew silent in their shared feelings of foreboding, anchored in disappointment. They feared losing their home, something that outweighed any guilt either of them felt about being treated any less inhumane as so many others with whom they shared a spiritual and physical bond.

Their prolonged silence turned apprehension led them into the living room and outside through the front door. Molly had grabbed a quilt off the couch to lay across both their laps. They made no sound. Sitting down on the handmade bench, their weary heads rested in the same direction, where cypress trees and grass-covered, blue-green hills met color-crossed foliage mixed with wildflowers. There—expansive grounds preceded a picturesque view which had been cultivated for farms, including their own, where several families grew large cotton crops, corn, and tobacco to sell. Some grew smaller crops of mustard greens, peas, carrots, and other vegetables to sustain themselves, and share with their neighbors.

The afternoon rain had dissipated, and the sun was breaking through. Its warmth enveloped them, and they threw off the quilt. Molly stroked Alex's temples and her pursed lips planted soft kisses above his eyes.

"Does that help some, baby?" Molly murmured, as she tried to ease her husband's tension. She added, "I never noticed the green speckles in your eyes."

He quipped, "Remember that famous painter who said the eyes are the window to the soul. I guess mine has some greenery in it, being that I'm a farmer and all."

"Stop, Alex, I'm not funning. I mean it, they're so clear with the sun on them." Molly said as she tugged at his sleeve. Through her husband's eyes, it was easy to see a future that was bright—for Alex, herself, the children. Alex looked down and clutched one of her small hands. He kissed each finger, then placed Molly's hands against the side of his face. In silence, they sat together on the short bench. Their bodies leaned together. In this moment, Molly felt hopeful again. From the front porch, she could hear the sweet voices of their little ones playing inside.

Like the scent of sweet mulberries, mingled with fallen pinecones that hung in the air after the rain, Molly promised herself that she would try to leave the murky, worrisome past behind, and look forward with hope to their future.

⤐

Alex didn't resent his neighbor Jim and his parents, but he couldn't stop thinking about how their situations differed. Did the Commission even call them up to Meridian to testify for their land?

"They want me to prove that I even deserve an inheritance."

Alex just wanted to tell those men, especially the ones with some Choctaw background, *"You're not making your society better by only including people like my neighbor Jim. He's probably 1/20th Indian; just about all white. But look at me, I'm like you. You must hate yourself, if you reject me. I'm more like you than he is."*

"Do you really expect them to?" Molly asked, when he told her of his thoughts.

"I dunno. Sometimes, I feel like I'm racing against the dash, Alex said.

Molly didn't know what Alex meant. But he explained it. "The dash is that tiny line they put on your tombstone between when you're born and when you die. It's made up of tiny pinpricks which represent our every moment, all clumped together. The dash is everything we do and what's done to us—all packed together to form one short line. I'm trying to add more specks into that dash before it finally cuts off."

Molly wondered aloud, *"And you wanna' get ahead of it?—the dash, I mean."*

"No," Alex said with a sigh. "I just want to add more to it. Better things, before it's all done."

20

ONLY THE CHOSEN FEW

FOUR MONTHS AFTER the Commission notified Alex they'd not made a ruling about his petition to own land in Indian Territory, the decision came. It was more than a year after he first testified in Meridian. Molly traveled to the postmaster to fetch the slim correspondence from the commission. When she got home, she placed the single page stamped "REJECTED" on the kitchen table for both of them to see. The one-page rejection had no details of the devastating decision, but then their attorney Hudson accessed a longer explanation of the ruling, and he presented that letter to them.

Rejection Notification Form- Alex's Mississippi Choctaw Application

Indian Commission Defends Decision to Reject the Powells

.W.
73

DEPARTMENT OF THE INTERIOR
COMMISSION TO THE FIVE CIVILIZED TRIBES

In the matter of the application of Anthony P. Powell
for the identification of himself and his thirteen
minor children, Charley H., Eveline, Joe, Eddie, Willie
Eugene, Clarence, Lesley, Henry, Ernest, Courtney,
Marshall, and Maude Powell, as Mississippi Choctaws,
M.C.R. 1625

DECISION

The record in this case shows that on April 4, 1901,
Anthony P. Powell appeared before the Commission at Meridian,
Mississippi, and there made personal application for the identification of himself and his thirteen minor children, Charley H.,
Eveline, Joe, Eddie, Willia, Eugene, Clarence, Lesley, Henry,
Ernest, Courtney, Marshall and Maude Powell as Mississippi Choctaws,
claiming to be descendants of Choctaw Indians who resided in the
state of Mississippi in 1830 and took advantage of the provisions
of article fourteen of the treaty made between the United States
government and the Choctaw tribe of Indians, concluded September
27, 1830, and known as the treaty of "Dancing Rabbit Creek." The
principal applicant claims descent from Alex Wilmer, an alleged full

-2-

blood Choctaw who married Fannie Powell, a negro woman, and who are
the parents of this applicant.

The record in this case further shows that the principal
applicant and his thirteen minor children for whom application is
made, have never been enrolled by the tribal authorities of the
Choctaw Nation as citizens of that tribe, or are their names found
upon any of the tribal rolls of the Choctaw Nation in the possession
of the Commission, nor have they ever been admitted to Choctaw
citizenship by a duly constituted court or committee of the Choctaw
Nation, or by the Commission to the Five Civilized Tribes, or by a
decree of the United States Court in Indian Territory, under the
provisions of the act of Congress of June 10, 1896(29 Stats. 321.)

The evidence offered in support of this application
aside from the oral statement of the principal applicant, embraces
the joint ex parte affidavit of Henry Tindall and James Dilling and
the ex parte affidavits of Richard Webb, Ed Williamson and D. H.
Tindall. By the oral statement of the principal applicant it is
attempted to be shown that he was born in the state of Mississippi
in about the year 1860 and has resided there all his life and is
an one half blood Choctaw. He does not attempt to trace his
alleged Choctaw blood any farther back than to his father, who he
alleges was a full blood Choctaw and a resident of Mississippi in
1830. He claims that his mother was a slave at the time his father
married her and for that reason she did not take the name of her
husband, and that he himself was always known by the name of his
mother. There is nothing in his testimony which tends to show that
any of his alleged Choctaw ancestors were ever recognized by the
Choctaw tribal authorities as members of the Choctaw tribe of
Indians in Mississippi, or that they complied or attempted to comply

-3-

with the provisions of article fourteen of the treaty of 1830. By
the joint ex parte affidavit of Henry Tindall and James Dilling,
it is attempted to be shown that affiants are acquainted with the
principal applicant and his wife and known that they were legally
married in the year 1879, and at the date of the making of this
applicationthey had had born to them and living the thirteen
children herein applied for. By the ex parte affidavits of Richard
Webb and Ed Williamson it is attempted to be shown that affiants
are acquainted with the principal applicant herein, and allege that
he is an one half blood Choctaw and recognized in the community in
which he resides as such, and that affiants were well acquainted
with his father and claim that he was a full blood Choctaw Indian.
By the ex parte affidavit of D. H. Tindall it is attempted to be
shown that he is acquainted with the principal applicant herein and
knows him to be the son of Alex Wilmer, an alleged full blood
Choctaw Indian and further states that at the time of the marriage
of said Alex Wilmer to the mother of the principal applicant ,
licenses were not procured by Indians and slaves, but they were
married under the customs existing at that time and by permission
of the master and mistress of the slave and that the children of
such marriages were usually known by the name of the mother. There
is nothing in any of these affidavits which tends to show that the
alleged Choctaw ancestors of the principal applicant, were ever
recognized members of the Choctaw tribe of Indians in Mississippi
or that they complied or attempted to comply with the provisions of
article fourteen of the treaty of 1830,

   The Commission in view of the fact that these applicants
have had sufficient time allowed them in which to present their

-4-

testimony considers this case as closed, and the only evidence
offered in support thereof is the oral statement of the principal
applicant and the documentary evidence filed by him, and by said
evidence it is attempted to be shown that the applicants herein
derive their alleged Choctaw blood from Alex Wilmer, father of the
principal applicant, who it is claimed was a full blood Choctaw.
In order for these applicants to be identified as Mississippi
Choctaws, it is incumbent upon them to show that they are descendants
of a Choctaw Indian who lived in Mississippi in 1830, and complied
or attempted to comply with the provisions of article fourteen of
the treaty of "Dancing Rabbit Creek" as the head of a family, or who
was the child of a recognized Choctaw head of a family who complied
for said child, or who was complied for as an orphan child of a
recognized Choctaw Indian. It is impossible to determine from the
evidence submitted whether Alex Wilmer, the father of the principal
applicant herein, and the remotest known alleged Choctaw ancestor of
these applicants, was living in Mississippi in 1830 as a recognized
Choctaw Indian, and complied or attempted to comply with the provisions of article fourteen of the treaty of 1830, and the only
search that can be made among the records of the Commission of those
persons who complied or attempted to comply with the provisions of
article fourteen of the treaty of 1830, is for the name of the
principal applicant's alleged father, and it does not appear from
said records that any person bearing said name ever signified his
intention to Colonel Wm. Ward, Indian Agent, Choctaw Agency, to
comply with the provisions of article fourteen, or presented his
claim as a beneficiary under said article to either of the Commis-
sions duly authorized by the acts of Congress of March 3, 1837 and
August 23, 1842, for the adjudication of such claims. Neither does
it appear from the records of the Commission to the Five Civilized

-8-

Tribes that there are affiliated with this case any other persons claiming descent or any rights as Choctaw Indians through Alex Wilmer, the alleged ancestor of the principal applicant herein.

The authority vested in the Commission by the twentyfirst section of the act of Congress of June 28, 1898(30 Stats. 495) is as follows:

"Said Commission shall have authority to determine the identity of Choctaw Indians claiming rights in the Choctaw lands under article fourteen of the treaty between the United States and the Choctaw Nation concluded September twenty-seventh, eighteen hundred and thirty, and to that end may administer oaths, examine witnesses, and perform all other acts necessary thereto and make report to the Secretary of the Interior."

It is the opinion of the Commission that the evidence in this case is insufficient to determine the identity of Anthony P. Powell, Charley E. Powell, Eveline Powell, Joe Powell, Eddie Powell, Willie Powell, Eugene Powell, Clarence Powell, Lesley Powell, Henry Powell, Ernest Powell, Courtney Powell, Marshall Powell and Maude Powell as Choctaw Indians entitled to rights in the Choctaw lands under the provision of law above quoted and that the application for their identification as such should be refused, and it is so ordered.

COMMISSION TO THE FIVE CIVILIZED TRIBES

Commissioners

Muskogee, Indian Territory.

APR 15 1902

The five page letter from the Commission detailed how Alex presented sworn affidavits from upstanding white citizens, such as Mr. Newman and his son (actual names in letter, *Henry* and *D.H. Tindall*); store owners Webb and Williamson, and Alex's friend and neighbor Jim, *James Dilling*. Even these sworn statements by white men in good standing, attesting to Alex's identity, wouldn't sway the Commission.

As a respected business and civic leader of Grenada County, Neuman (Tindall) could have jeopardized his long- standing position in the community when he stood up for Alex and Molly by presenting this letter:

> "*A number of years ago, I was well and personally acquainted with Alex Wilmer, a full-blood Choctaw Indian, and Alex P. Powell, his son. I know that Alex Wilmer lived with the mother of A.P. Powell, as her husband, up to the time of his death. At that time, licenses were not procured by Indians and slaves, but they were married under the existing customs and by permission of the master or mistress of the slave, and that the children were usually known by the name of the mother. This way, the said Alex P. Powell named herein, has always been known.*"

Alex would never forget how Mr. Neuman (Tindall) and his son put their reputation on the line in that affidavit, confirming his friendship with Alex's father and vouching for his Choctaw heritage.

Heartbroken, Alex made another appeal on May 2, 1902. In just over two weeks later, he received another rejection letter. Feeling that the actual law and God were on his side, Alex respectfully wrote another letter of appeal to the Commission on June 9. With an even quicker letter of response, the Commission again denied Alex's request.

That didn't stop Alex. Expecting to receive a letter of

rejection each time; he had an appeal letter already prepared. Alex even included additional affidavits to prove his ancestry, which he could trace back to his great grandfather.

It took the Commission only five days to reject his latest appeal and proof. He was convinced that with each of his letters, the Commission was growing more callous.

Desperate, Alex finally implored his attorneys to go directly to the Secretary of the Interior. It worked. They agreed to let Alex submit his deposition. This time, after months of no mention of a court date, Alex sent out another letter to the Commission on May 20, 1903. He notified them of the secretary's intentions. Alex also introduced a physical witness willing to testify on his behalf.

The last two rejection letters Alex would receive came on May 27 and on June 3. The Commission denied knowledge of a promise from the Secretary of the Interior to Mr. Powell. They also refused the introduction of any new evidence. With this, the Commission declared Alex's case closed.

In a way, Alex felt relieved. The process, including making relentless appeals, had been long, wrenching and filled with disappointment. By now, he knew that it was time to end his tiring pursuit for land, and his good fight.

Alex stayed in town the rest of the day to hide his pain and despair from Molly and the children. He realized that he couldn't save them from being forced out.

PART IV

21

PRAYER FOR THE POWELLS

LEX AND MOLLY Powell, and their 15 children, had packed up all their belongings; they were on their way, even without the promise of land of their own. They had to leave many of their cherished items, including furniture, behind. The carrier, known as L. P. Hutchinson, orchestrated their excursion. It would carry the young family to their final destination in Homer, Oklahoma, near Ardmore.

The trip was grueling. It made some of the children sick to their stomachs. Molly did her best to get them to the top, up on deck, to throw up over the sides of the railings. It was a scene that repeated, over and over. The sounds and scents they experienced on the journey were new and sometimes overwhelming. Having to be packed in together like cattle on the boat was horrible. As they made their way, there was very little to eat. And there was no civilized way to relieve themselves when needed.

Upon arrival, it took a week to get the entire family from a holding station to a permanent place to live in the town of

Homer. Their house was half the size of the one they'd left in Mississippi, and not half as nice. There was only a lone Shumard Oak out back to lend any beauty and shade.

The town, larger than Misterton, but not nearly as picturesque, was situated about 10 miles south of the Arbuckle Mountains, in southern Oklahoma. It was characterized by ridges visible within the shoreline of several lakes.

Previously Congress had established this Oklahoma Territory of unoccupied lands in Indian Territory. It was exclusively for Native Americans in the East who were forced from their lands. The Oklahoma Organic Act of 1890 created an organized, incorporated territory of the United States of Oklahoma Territory. Its intent was to combine the Oklahoma and Indian territories into a single State of Oklahoma.

Alex's ancestors had gradually ceded most of their lands in the Southeast section of the U.S. through a series of treaties. The southern part of Indian Country (what eventually became the State of Oklahoma) served as the destination for the policy of Indian removal which had been aggressively pursued by President Andrew Jackson after the passage of the Indian Removal Act of 1830. It was being enforced again by the current president. The forced trail ended in Oklahoma Territory, where there were already many Indians living as well as whites and escaped slaves.

Despite all that had happened, the Powells continued to hold on to God's love for their family. Alex understood the depth of his wife's pain and sadness. He appreciated how she cleverly hid it beneath the strength and love she showered on them. Molly had an unselfish heart. When they first arrived, to lighten their load, she shared with the children, who were seeing snow for the first time, her own reaction when she saw it in Boston, as a girl.

"*The snow began just before Christmas. There was a chill in the air. And when the sun rose, it would bounce off the fresh mounds of snow like diamonds. I loved to hear it crunch beneath my feet.*"

The Powell family was determined to put on their

bravest face to weather this latest storm, a burden they called their *tribulation.*

๙

Alex, who had prayed for so long, still couldn't understand why this was happening to him. Although he kept praying, this situation brought him to one conclusion. No more allowing those who controlled everything, to change him to fit into their mold they set out for him; while they still deny him his right-ful identity and heritage, despite his efforts. *Why did every step he and his ancestors take have to be scrutinized?* He asked God.

Those Commission men were well aware that everything doesn't line up perfectly in anyone's life… that's no reason to take away what a man has always had and depended on for sur-vival. Alex believed, if every "t" was to have been crossed and every "i" dotted, it still would not satisfy the Commission of Indian Affairs, in his case. Jim and his parents, who had been Alex's friends and neighbors, shared that the government men took their own information without even referring to the Indian rolls, then went ahead and added their names to it. Alex found it difficult to accept that, since for him, nothing ever pleased the Commission, no matter how accurately it was presented.

Before giving up, Alex pledged to God and himself that he would tell his story, time and time again, and prayed that someone would listen.

So, on Oct. 20, 1903, looking out at the lone tree in the back of the house, Alex sat down at his desk to write another plea directly to W.A. Jones, Commissioner of the Secretary of the Interior. It didn't matter that the secretary's office insisted that he give up the fight. This time their consideration took longer than before—a whole 37 days. But without fail, on November 28, Alex was denied for the seventh time.

Commission Rejects Ancestry through Alex's Grandfather

(COPY).

DEPARTMENT OF THE INTERIOR,

OFFICE OF INDIAN AFFAIRS,

Washington, Nov. 7, 1903.

Land.
70252-1903.

The Honorable,

The Secretary of the Interior.

Sir:

I have the honor to acknowledge receipt of Departmental letter of the 27th ultimo, (I.T.D. 9271-1903), enclosing letter from Mr. A. P. Powell, Tattums, Indian Territory, relative to his application for identification as a Mississippi Choctaw, which was denied by the Department on May 21, 1902. With his letter Mr. Powell submitted affidavit of himself and joint affidavit of Mink Love and Viney Love in support of his request for a rehearing in this case.

It appears from the papers that the ancestor from whom Mr. Powell claims descent was a Choctaw Indian named Tuk-e-lubbee, and referring to a list of names of Choctaws to whom script was issued under the Fourteenth Article of the Treaty of Dancing Rabbit Creek, prepared by this office, the Department invites attention to the fact that this list shows there was a person named Tuk-a-lubbee to whom script was issued under the Provisions

-2-

of Article 14 of the Choctaw Treaty of 1830. The office is requested to consider these papers in connection with the record in the case, and furnish the Department with the material part of the testimony taken in connection with the original case of Tuk-a-lubbee together with a recommendation as to a rehearing.

Mink Love and Viney Love swear in their affidavit that from their childhood to the time they left Mississippi with the Choctaws they knew a full blood Choctaw Indian named Tuk-e-lubbee, who at the date of the treaty had several children, among whom was a son named Alexander Wilmer. A. P. Powell claims to obtain his Choctaw blood from Tuk-e-lubbee through his father, Alexander Wilmer.

The Tuk-a-lubbee whose name appears in the list of Choctaw Indians to whom script was issued under the Fourteenth Article of the Choctaw Treaty of 1830, was a son of Shik-a-pan-o-wa. The testimony in connection with his case was taken on the 3rd day of April, 1838, by Commissioners Vroom and Barton. The testimony of the head of the family is to the effect that in 1830 he lived on Heth-tok-fo-li-a, (Beaver Pond), and had a wife and seven children living with him, all the children being unmarried. The sixth child was named Tuk-a-lubbee, a male, eleven years of age at the time the testimony was taken, making him three years of age in 1830. Tuk-a-lubbee had a twin brother named Pis-a-tubbee.

-3-

From the statements made by the witnesses, which are proposed to be used in Mr. Powell's behalf, it is evident the Tuk-e-lubbee they refer to is not the Tuk-a-lubbee in behalf of whom script was issued, under the Fourteenth Article of the Choctaw Treaty. The Indian they refer to was an adult and the head of a family at at that time, and the actual beneficiary under the Fourteenth Article was a child of three years.

An examination of the records of this office has been made with reference to other persons of the same or similar name, and it is discovered that no person of a simialar name was either an applicant for benefits under the Fourteenth Article or a beneficiary thereunder.

I am therefore of opinion that the reopening of the case as prayed by Mr. Powell should not be granted, since it would only be an expenditure of money by him without profit.

Copy of the deposition in the case referred to is inclosed.

Very respectfully,

W. A. Jones,
Commissioner.

E.B.H.-L.C.

Alex, the man, fought hard to focus on his beleaguered family, and not the irony of the situation. First, they find his grandfather's name on the rolls, then they can't find him, and now they supposedly find him, but he's three years old!

Why couldn't previous affidavits from four upstanding white men—community leaders who knew him all his life, and even those who knew his father as a Choctaw, knew his wife and children, and now Mink and Vinny who knew his grandfather—satisfy these men?

He was well aware that the original land, Muskogee, Indian Territory, on which a decision of his eligibility for land rights was to be rendered by the Indian Commission, was previously inhabited by his father's people, the Choctaw Native Americans. It was obtained by the United States under the terms of the Treaty of Dancing Rabbit Creek in 1830, during the period of Indian removal. After the treaty was ratified, European-American settlers began to move into the area. And now they are determined to keep him and his family off of any land to replace what has been wrenched from him.

He also couldn't ignore those shifty "insurance men" who had been scurrying around Misterton and now Homer. What did they want? He had an idea. Although Alex had gathered some information about the men, and wondered if they were somehow connected with the government, he couldn't prove it. When he'd heard that his old friend and neighbor Ed Carter had disappeared, Alex wondered if he had been drinking or did something else happen? After sending comforting words to his children, Alex had no time to look into his friend's disappearance. No, he didn't have that luxury. Outside of work, his every waking moment was filled with trying to get this Commission of Indian Affairs more evidence. His mind had blotted out the last letter demanding that he stop trying. His family was living in Indian Territory without a home to call their own. They'd been given no other alternative but to come west, leaving behind the security of his possession through his forefathers.

22
THE HIGH AND MIGHTY

BLANKETED WITH MIST, in a succession of fall mornings, crisp scarlet leaves were little more than a red haze. A blurry view of several small acorns shared the ground's surface. Staring high above the trees, Alex squinted at the smoky sky, blanketed with the same grey clouds of yesterday. Yet the atmosphere was part of the new landscape, since his and Molly's once comfortable home, tucked away behind welcoming mulberry and pecan trees—was no more. The weathered brown structure in which he and his family now resided was a far cry from the home they'd left behind in Grenada County, Mississippi. Alex had renovated that home for his family. It sat on the same land where he's spent part of his childhood.

This new landscape was located within several different regions, including the Arbuckle Mountains, the Coastal Plains, the Redbed Plains (a sub-region of the Osage Plains), and the Cross Timbers. The land varied from vigorous hills to rolling prairies to flat bottomlands. Just miles away, the Washita River, Caddo Creek, and their tributaries drained the northern portion of the county, and several creeks fed into the Red River. Two cotton gins, a blacksmith shop, and a general store served the surrounding area. Squeezed against the backdrop of this colder, less picture-perfect scene, the Powells had sufficed for over a year.

✺

After multiple rejections, and the denial of yet another rehearing, Alex fought back again in 1904, with an appeal directly to the Secretary of the Interior to which the Commission responded early the next year. He'd gone to Coop and Luckett, a well-known law firm in Washington D.C., with hopes that they would be able to get him the justice he was seeking, especially after learning that "insurance men" had again returned having neighbors who couldn't read or write sign mysterious papers .

After hearing the details of Alex's story, they took on the case for a minimal fee. When Molly learned from Alex's attorney about the latest ruling, she didn't know what to believe about all those so-called honorable men on the Commission. As for the names on the affidavits Alex gave this time around, some of the gentlemen she knew, but others she didn't. Although Molly wasn't familiar with all the men listed who provided additional affidavits, she knew most of them, and they were honest people. She was well acquainted with Alex's father's background, but she had no notion of the many Indian rolls mentioned by the Commission in this pre-ruling letter. Molly only knew of the original roll that included his father's name. At least, that's what Alex was told. He learned about the roll when they lived in Mississippi. But this time, in their response on December 2, 1904, the Commission denied that Indian roll ever existed.

Secretary of the Interior Denies Existence of Missing Rolls

Muskogee, Indian Territory, December 2, 1904.

The Honorable

The Secretary of the Interior,

Sir:

Receipt is hereby acknowledged of Departmental communication of October 22, 1904, (I. T. D. 0825-1904) transmitting, for report and recommendation, letter of Messrs. Copp & Luckett of October 19, 1904, with which was inclosed reply brief in the Choctaw enrollment case of A. P. Powell, et al. Therein Messrs. Copp & Luckett refer to certain citizenship rolls of the Choctaw Nation on which it is alleged the name of the father of said A. P. Powell appears, and the Department directs that if these rolls are not in the possession of the Commission, thorough search be made therefor as early as practicable.

Reporting in this matter I have the honor to advise that in neither the letter of Copp & Luckett nor in the letter of Powell, to which reference is made in said brief and in which a copy appears, is any definite statement made as to what rolls of the Choctaw Nation are referred to by applicant.

I have further to report that there are in the possession of the Commission the 1885 census roll of the Choctaw Nation, the 1893 leased district payment roll and the 1896 census roll of said

2

nation, and that thorough search has been made, on various occasions,
and the officials and ex-officials of the Choctaw Nation have all
been visited in the attempt to discover the existence of any other
rolls which may have been made by the Choctaw tribal authorities, but
all such efforts have been fruitless, and I know of no other rolls
of the Choctaw Nation in the possession of the tribal authorities or
the attorneys for the Choctaw and Chickasaw nations.

The communication of Messrs. Copp & Luckot, together with
the inclosure, is herewith returned.

Respectfully,

Chairman.

AD 14-2

Through the Commissioner
of Indian Affairs.

Armed with pages of evidence and affidavits, along with his
attorneys, Alex hadn't been bracing for yet another setback. He
told Molly he'd done everything the Commission asked, and a
denial this time would be almost too much to bear. So, he put it
out of his mind, and tried to get into the spirit of the holidays.

Molly and the older children had leafy red poinsettias in
green wicker baskets scattered around the living room. To
add to the décor, the girls lit two long pillar candles for each
window, and placed glass holders with snowflake designs over
them. They popped corn and strung cranberries around the
room, reminding everyone of the lively celebrations they had in
years past. There was even pie, although pecans were harder to

come by now, the women managed to somehow piece together a pie with the sweet nutty flavor and aroma he remembered. Together, they sang the children's favorites, "The First Noel," with the pot-bellied stove burning in the corner of the room. The only thing missing was their traditional Christmas tree, but as long as they were together, nothing else mattered.

"Let's sing *Away in a Manager* or *O Little Town of Bethlehem.* I like those more." In high spirits, the children argued over which song was best. And before long, they were, shoving one another into the poinsettia plants scattered around the room.

Once past the holidays and the New Year, there was yet another setback. It felt insurmountable to Alex. Shuttered in the bedroom with his wife pushing the door closed, he held a copy of the five-page letter and began to read it.

"I had always b-believed," he stammered, "and I still do, in how the Bible says, 'He won't p-put more on you than you can bear.'" Alex then crumpled the pages in his hands and wept quietly in front of his partner, while Molly held on and comforted him. They prayed the contrast between the warm, happy scene in the front room and despair in their bedroom would soon end.

Alex picked up the pages that had dropped to the floor, and noticed they continued to refer him as Anthony. The letter also mentioned several names of the additional thirteen upstanding, well-known citizens who stepped forward to support him—and put their reputation on the line. The sacrifice of so many others, in the midst of continuous, unrelenting obstacles, brought both husband and wife to fresh tears. This time neither held back.

Department of Interior Rejects All 13 Sworn Affidavits; Upholds Indian Commission's Original Ruling

C O P Y.

D. C. #5655.   W.C.F.

D E P A R T M E N T   O F   T H E   I N T E R I O R,
                                                                                   FHE.
                              W a s h i n g t o n.
I.T.D. 7716-8295-9487-1904.
          10483-12530- "   January 30, 1905.
L. R. S.

Commission to the Five Civilized Tribes,

          Muskogee, Indian Territory.

Gentlemen:

          The Department has considered a motion submitted by
the attorneys for the applicants in the Mississippi Choctaw
case of Anthony P. Powell, et al, to have the application made
by the applicants for identification as Mississippi Choctaws
considered as an application for enrollment as Choctaws by
blood.

          You rejected the applicants April 15, 1902, and on
May 21, 1902, your decision was affirmed by the Department.

          November 16, 1903, the Department denied a motion for
a rehearing of the case.

          It appears that the principal applicant claims descent
through his father, Alexander Wilmer, from a full blood Choctaw
named Tukelubbee, who, it is claimed, was the head of a Choctaw
family and the father of several children in 1830, and a beneficiary under article 14 of the Choctaw treaty of 1830.

          It appears from the report of the Commissioner of

(2)

Indian Affairs of November 7, 1903, that one Tukelubbee, who was a beneficiary under article 14 of the Choctaw treaty of 1830, was a child three years of age at the date of the treaty.

The principal applicant sets out in his affidavit that at the time of his original application for identification as a Mississippi Choctaw his attorney failed to inform him correctly as to the proper basis for such an application.

There are submitted in support of the motion affidavits of W. M. Smith, B. Pettis, and W. C. Franklin, to the effect that Tukelubbee, the grandfather of Anthony P. Powell, was a part Choctaw Indian, living in Mississippi at the time of the adoption of the treaty of 1830; that in the year 1848 or 1849, said Tukelubbee went to the Indian Territory, where he settled and remained up to the time of his death about 20 years later.

The attorneys for the Nation submitted certain affidavits in support of their contention that the motion should not be granted, among them being the affidavits of Robert Pettis, and J. L. Smith, said to be known as "Bill Smith."

On October 22, 1904, the Department referred to you a communication from Copp & Luckett, of this city, dated October 19, 1904, transmitting a reply brief in this case, and referring to certain citizenship rolls of the Choctaw Nation on which it is alleged that the name of the father of Anthony P. Powell

(3)

appears, which rolls, it appears, the applicants were unable
to find. You were directed to make a thorough search of the
rolls referred to. On December 2, 1904, you reported in the
matter, stating that neither the letter of Messrs. Copp & Luckett, or that of Mr. Powell, which was incorporated in the brief
referred to you, contain a definite statement as to what rolls
of the Choctaw Nation are referred to by the applicants; that
the Commission have in their possession the 1885 census roll
of the Choctaw Nation, the 1893 Leased District Payment Roll,
and the 1896 census roll of the Nation, and that a thorough
search has been made at diverse times; that officials and
ex-officials of the Choctaw Nation have been visited with a
view to discovering the existence of any other rolls which
may have been made by the tribal authorities; that such efforts have not met with success, and that the Commission knows
of no other rolls of the Choctaw Nation in the possession of
the tribal authorities or the attorneys for the Choctaw and
Chickasaw Nations.

The Department considers it unnecessary to pass upon
the question discussed by the attorneys for both sides as to
the credit to be given the statements contained in certain of
the affidavits submitted. Section 21 of the act of June 28,
1898 (30 Stat., 495), provides:

(4)

"Said commission is authorized and directed to make correct rolls of the citizens by blood of all the other tribes, eliminating from the tribal rolls such names as may have been placed thereon by fraud or without authority of law, enrolling such only as may have lawful right thereto, and their descendants born since such rolls were made, with such intermarried white persons as may be entitled to Choctaw and Chickasaw citizenship under the treaties and the laws of said tribes."

The Act of Congress approved May 31, 1900 (31 Stat., 221), provides that the Commission-

"shall not receive, consider, or make any record of any application of any person for enrollment as a member of any tribe in Indian Territory who has not been a recognized citizen thereof, and duly and lawfully enrolled or admitted as such, and its refusal of such applications shall be final when approved by the Secretary of the Interior."

The Act of Congress approved July 1, 1902 (32 Stat., 641), incorporated the provisions of the acts above quoted, section 27 thereof providing that-

"The rolls of the Choctaw and Chickasaw citizens and Choctaw and Chickasaw freedmen shall be made by the Commission to the Five Civilized Tribes, in strict compliance with the act of Congress approved June 28, 1898 (30 Stats., 495), and the act of Congress approved May 31, 1900 (31 Stats., 221), except as herein otherwise provided."

Inasmuch as it is not shown by the affidavits submitted that the applicants have been recognized citizens of the Choctaw Nation, or that they have been duly and lawfully enrolled or admitted as such, or that they are the descendants of persons whose names appear on the rolls of the Choctaw Nation, the Department does not feel warranted, in view of the provisions of the acts above quoted, in granting the motion of

(5)

the applicants; the same is therefore hereby denied, and you will so notify the parties concerned.

> Respectfully,
>
> THOS RYAN
>
> Acting Secretary.

23

Navigating Unfamiliar Territory

NOTHER YEAR HAD passed in a place where the days moved sluggishly and where nothing was the same as before. The weather conditions were undependable, the winds relentless, and the land was too dry for fruitful planting. As the children grew, most of the older ones spent their days cultivating the farmstead and caring for their younger brothers and sisters. Molly and the eldest daughters spent their days doing laundry— hanging their garments across three clotheslines out back. They also cooked and cleaned. Alex spent long hours divided between working the field outside and getting his words down on paper, trying to recall his testimony in Meridian, and new information he'd gathered since he first began his fight.

Thrust into a new land, there were so many changes underway in the place where the Powells now lived. Other citizens of Indian Territory would try this year—to gain admission to the union as the State of Sequoyah—but would be rebuffed by Congress and an Administration, which did not want two new Western states, Sequoyah and Oklahoma. President Theodore

Roosevelt then proposed a compromise that would join Indian Territory with Oklahoma Territory to form a single state. This resulted in passage of the Oklahoma Enabling Act in 1906, which the president signed the next year. It empowered the people residing in Indian Territory and Oklahoma Territory to elect delegates to a state constitutional convention. However, none of these details had any place in Alex and Molly's life, where their own future plans had become muddled and unclear.

This particular day, the morning started out with promise. They had days like this when they lived in Mississippi, where the bright sun was out most all the time and the willow-oak branches swayed gently. These moments helped chase away unpleasant thoughts from everyone's minds. By the afternoon, the day turned somber, like gray storm clouds, as Alex wrestled with how to prove his Indian ancestry.

∿

It was a warm, late, February afternoon in Ardmore, just outside of Homer. Alex was still learning about this new land on which he was forced to settle. By the end of the last century, years before their family arrived in Oklahoma, this community was on its way to becoming one of the main cities in Oklahoma, then disaster struck with a fire that destroyed downtown. Then, just when they'd arrived in the early 1900's, a deadly explosion destroyed most of the city, so the town was still rebuilding.

This month, March, the year 1907, proved to be one of the hottest as the temperature shot up to 60 degrees. The unseasonal weather coincided with signs of renewed hope. The song of a gold-blue, winged lark perched on the longest branch of the oak tree out back floated through the window. Its tiny bent legs and feet, stiffly curled on the longest branch, as his tiny eyes opened and shut.

Alex's mission was rekindled with the promise of more solid corroborating witnesses. That morning, he tucked away his heavy overcoat, and threw on a lightweight cover, to accompany them on the long walk to and from town.

"Moll, I walked over with Old Joe, Martha and a few others who also made the journey here from Grenada. Those two especially, since they've been around so long, and Joe's outlived everyone. He and Martha agreed to give a statement for us."

Molly had been putting away the dried, folded clothes on the bed. She sighed, "Haven't we already done that–many times over?"

Purposely ignoring his wife's comment, Alex carefully removed two official sheets from a large mailing envelope.

"It's different. They both have been around for so long, especially Joe," he said, making an effort not to argue. "I believe he may have misplaced a few of the names in his head, but my lawyer, Yancy said we need to get more people to give their word for us who actually knew my Pa, and our connection to the Choctaw."

"Is that Joe and Martha's words to the notary?" Molly asked, reaching for the letters in her husband's hand. "I'll be careful," she added.

"I'll let you see it, wait a second, please be gentle with it. They had to have it written word for word, and Yancy said it cost me two bits each just to get this."

"Didn't I tell you I'd be careful," she insisted, sliding her hand under the first, printed page and placing it on her lap.

After she took it, "Here's the other one," he said, adding, "Yancy met Martha and Old Joe and me over to the notary in Ardmore to get these prepared. He's going to send them off tomorrow, along with mine."

Ardmore, Indian Territory.

Southern District.

I, Martha Jamison, being first duly sworn, state on oath that I am about 85 years old; that I know A. P. Powell, and knew his mother, Fannie Potubbee; also knew his mother's father, who was called Potubbee. Potubbee was said to have been a son of Oklahoma or Oslotenot. I also knew A. P. Powell's father's father, who was known as Tukelubbee. A. P. Powell's father was named Alexander Wilmer. They all lived in old Choctaw County, Mississippi. They were always recognized as Indians and members of the Choctaw Tribe, spoke the Indian language and it was always said they had received land in Mississippi under the Treaty of 1830, which Treaty I believe was called the Treaty of Dancing Rabbit Creek. I am no kin to A. P. Powell and have no interest in this cause whatever.

her

(Signed) MARTHA X JAMISON.

mark.

Witnesses to mark:

(Signed) OLA HALLOWAY.

(Signed) ROBERT E. LEE.

Subscribed and sworn to before me on this 12th day of February, 1907.

(Signed) OLA HALLOWAY

Notary Public.

(Notarial Seal)

Additional Sworn Affidavits confirming Indian Ancestry

Ardmore, Indian Territory.

  Southern District.

    I, Joe Jamison, being first duly sworn, state on oath that I am about 89 or 90 years of age; that I know A. P. Powell and have known him a great many years. I knew him in Mississippi and also knew his family, including his old grand father, Tukelubbee, who was the father of Alexander Wilmer. I also knew Potubbee, who was A. P. Powell's grandfather, on his mother's side. I also knew Fannie Potubbee, the mother of A. P. Powell, and Susan Buckner, A. P. Powell's mother's mother. Susan Buckner was said to have been a Portugese woman. His other ancestry on both sides were Mississippi Choctaw Indians, and it was always said and known over the country generally that they had complied with the Treaty of 1830, on which they got land.

    I am no kin to A. P. Powell and have no interest in this matter.

                 (Signed) JOE JAMISON   His X mark.

Witnesses to Mark:

    (Signed) OLA HALLOWAY.

    (Signed) ROBERT E. LEE.

  Subscribed and sworn to before me on this 12th day of February, 1907.

                (Signed) OLA HALLOWAY

                      Notary Public.

(Notarial Seal)

Molly took in every word on both papers and commented, "This one mentions your mother. And it says that she was a slave, but it doesn't say she was mixed with white."

She then asked, "Do you think you should send it?"

"All I know is her people came from Virginia, she mentioned some Portuguese and some Indian, but I know more about my Pa's people than hers."

"Maybe you should search for a few more old-timers to see if anybody remembers her people."

"Not now, there's no time. I don't think I need to do any more than I already have here. I suspect all this mailing is costing money that we don't have left to spend."

Molly finished re-reading and put both statements back inside the envelope. She then slipped her fingers into those of her tired, restless husband. His hand was noticeably shaking as he took the package from her.

"Please baby, don't worry," she said, "I know you're worn out. I'm so sorry for being snippy earlier."

She rubbed her palm against the back of his sturdy neck. She could feel the hard, tense muscles beneath. Leaning over, she whispered in his ear. "You will always be my strong fella and a good provider—no one can take that away from you in my eyes."

He patted her hand and reached across the wood table. "I want you to take a look at this," he said, "It's my statement. I'm sending it certified at the same time as Joe and Martha's."

"Gentle now, don't bend it." He added, handing it over. "I promise, I won't," she assured him without snapping this time, but somewhat disappointed that he hadn't sufficiently acknowledged her show of love and support.

Notary Confirming Alex Powell's Ancestral Ties

Ardmore, Indian Territory.

    Southern District.

    I, A. P. Powell, being first duly sworn, state on oath that since testifying before the Dawes Commission at Meridian, Mississippi, I have ascertained beyond question that I am a direct lineal descendant from one Tukelubbee on my father's side and from one Potubbee on my mother's side, both of whom were Mississippi Choctaw Indians and both complied with or attempted to comply with the Treaty of 1830.

    My grandfather, Tukelubbee, when I was a small boy and living with my parents in old Choctaw County, Mississippi, gave me a small pony named "Spatt". I remember this incident well. My father, Alexander Wilmer, had left home a short time prior to this incident and stated that he was going west to see his father, Tukelubbee. On their return to old Choctaw County, Mississippi, my grandfather made me a present of this pony. I have never seen the old man, my grandfather, Tukelubbee, since this incident. He stated that he was going back west to his home to live. I have also ascertained that old man Tukelubbee, my grandfather, was buried at Old Boggy, in the Choctaw Nation, Indian Territory.

    Potubbee was my mother's father. My mother was named Fannie Potubbee. Susan Wilmer was Tukelubbee's wife, and my grandmother. I remember to have heard Susan Wilmer say that she went to Commissioner Ward for the purpose of registering and that Ward cursed her and that she and her family, the Wilmers, had a fuss with Commissioner Ward and that Commissioner Ward would never enroll these Indians after this incident.

    I advised Mr. Hudson, at Meridian, Miss., who was then my attorney, in 1901, and he advised me not to trace my ancestry no further than my father. For this reason the full statement of facts does not appear in my testimony taken by the Commission at Meridian, Mississippi, on April 4, 1901.

              (Signed) A. P. POWELL.

    Subscribed and sworn to before me on this 12th day of

February, 1907.

              (Signed) OLA HALLOWAY

                      Notary Public.

(Notarial Seal)

                (COPY)

In his written statement, Alex left out the memory he had of a comment his father made regarding his own parents before he died. His father had said, "You know we didn't talk about such things." But Alex never forgot his father commenting that his mother was known to be an exquisitely beautiful woman, but she stayed faithful to her husband [Tukeelubee], and they had to suffer the consequences for it. He'd said, "She chose to fight off the attention of many high falutin men."

"And now they say they can't find her or my Grandfather Tukeelubee's names on the 1830 Dancing Creek Treaty," Alex thought.

Later he shared that delicate information he'd kept from Molly. "It's what the old people think may have happened, cause nothing else explains it, unless there's some other names listed that are on missing pages no one knows about. It's a far- fetched notion, but the old-timers believe she was such a proud woman that they left her and her husband's name off to repay her for fighting off their advances. But this still couldn't explain why the Commission keeps rejecting me, given all that I've provided them."

᠊ᢒ᠊

Later that evening, Molly brought up the old-timer's statements again, "Why isn't Old Joe's statement enough to go with yours? Why do they need one from Martha, too?"

Alex could answer easily, since no matter what he was doing at any time, his struggle was never far from his mind.

"I learned since giving testimony in Meridian that not only will they not trust just my word, but they won't trust it with only a few people backing me up," Alex said, " Each time I appeal, I need as many as are willing to confirm that I am the son and grandson of who I say I am. I couldn't do without Martha. She knew my Pa's people, but she also knew my mother's people from way back. She even knew my mother's father. I never got to meet them, like I did my father's Pa. And I was only a little boy then. I just remember seeing that he was tall—taller than my father. And he had a rough, reddish brown face like the side of a cedar tree."

He continued, "Only problem is you know Joe and Martha couldn't read or write, so they had to say the words to the notary, and he had to write down what they said. And you know how the old timers get nervous talking in front of white folks, especially since they came west to this Oklahoma Indian Territory; always afraid their words are going to be misinterpreted or written down wrong like in the old days. I asked if I could just help them write it, and then go to the notary for the signatures, but I'll do whatever Yancy says. And he said, I couldn't write it down for them, it was only official, legal-like, if they were to say it in front of the notary.

Molly listened while removing pins from her hair, undoing several long graying strands nestled between chestnut- colored waves. The tight twist that held her waist length hair in order during long, busy days had been piled to one side of her head.

"But you know I should have never listened to my old attorney, Hudson," Alex moaned, "I still don't know his reason for having me not tell those men in Meridian everything I knew about my people. For some reason, he said if I knew my grandfather, and found out he wasn't really Choctaw, then I wouldn't have a chance. Now, it makes me look bad in front of these men, and on top of it, my original attorney Hudson is nowhere to be found. He could admit that he was the one who told me to keep my mouth shut."

Molly placed her hairpins on the side table.

"I wish I'd known he told you to do that. I would have said you might as well tell all the truth than part of it, 'cause you will only get caught up not remembering just how much of the truth you left out." She added, "And half-truths can make you look like a liar. I'm just glad that the half-truth–that you couldn't read—didn't cause a problem. I guess they understood what you meant. "

"Well, we can't change things now," Alex said, "So I'm just going to keep trying to get them to allow me to speak on what I've found out and what I already knew then."

"I'd go with you, but I need to go to town tomorrow for the month's supplies. So, I need time to stand in front of the looking glass–clean up, comb my hair and get this tired look off my face. I'm getting a head start tonight." She said, still fussing with her hair.

"Why so much?" he asked.

She quipped, "One must be presentable to the ladies for judging."

Alex laughed freely at her take on folk's ways. His Molly hadn't changed, in spite of everything.

"Good night." They said in unison.

24

WINTER WARMTH
AND VANITY

T HE UNUSUALLY LATE winter warmth of 1907 brought no so such change in the Powell's predicament. Each time Alex had given the Commission what they asked for, they'd ask him for something else. A great number of upstanding men who knew Alex in the community continued to come, asking if they could help in some way. Affidavits had come from men like Bob Pettis, Bill Smith, Franklin, Johnston, Austin Kelly—men who knew Alex all his life, or his mother, father, and their backgrounds.

"Baby, we've been trying for seven years now, and we still can't get them to do right by us," Molly said, standing over the pressing board, finishing her husband's trousers, with her 18-month-old resting against her hip.

While reaching for his pants, Alex leaned over and noticed the thickening veins developing in his wife's legs. It came from carrying so many children.

Catching him eyeing her legs, Molly became self- conscious without meaning to and expressed thoughts she'd been holding inside.

"It's been five years since we had to leave Mississippi, and we're still trying to prove who you are to those government men to have them relinquish their hold on your father's inheritance–our land. There comes a time when we have to face the truth and move on." She stated firmly. "I know we don't have what we had before, but the children can't grow up believing in something that we can't make happen, no matter how hard we work and pray."

Forgetting his trousers, her husband held his palms out in front of him, stared down at them, before cupping his face in his hands. He stood like this for several moments.

"Alex, do you hear me, baby? Alex?"

Molly put down the pressing iron when he sat down without responding.

Alex was thinking about his old friend and notary Ed Carter. He never forgot how the man disappeared in the woods in back of his own house. Alex still wondered if he had been drinking or did something else happen?

"What?" He stared in Molly's direction without seeing her.

Next, without warning, he jumped up, thrust his chair back, and pounded out a declaration with his right hand against his chest.

"This here man has got to keep going! Do you hear me, Moll? I can't go on if you're not with me. I need for you to believe in me, 'cause I can see what's ahead. I'll get what's mine—for you and the children. Just believe that I can do it. Molly, please," Alex begged.

Blaming herself for allowing suppressed vanity to get the best of her, Molly hunched her shoulders, bowed and backed away dragging her ailing foot, which became heavy again, after all these years. She was only a child when the illness first hit her. At times, it temporarily weakened her left ankle and foot if she became overwrought.

"I will make it happen, Molly," he continued to shout, "It's just gonna take more thinking on my part and more praying on yours."

With the littlest one still at her side, she reached around for the closed bedroom door behind her and cried, "I know you will baby… I'm sorry. But Lord help me… I'm just so doggone tired."

With the shut door between them, he hollered more to himself than her.

"I know, Molly! I know you are. I am too. But let's just thank God we've got each other and old friends still praying and backing us up!"

Alex pulled out his handkerchief and wiped his face. Without another sound, he hung the tan trousers his wife had pressed over the spindle back chair, pulled on his worn overalls, and headed outside to the field.

25

A New Man takes the Helm

WEEKS EARLIER AS the unseasonal warmth began, and before the sheriff showed up on their doorstep, Alex found their newest attorney, who went through all the Commission paperwork back to 1900. He told Alex he could help.

"Moll, this new attorney, Yancy said he wanted to send his own letter of introduction along with those I showed you of Old Joe's and Martha's–and mine, of course. So, I am going back to his office tomorrow to take these so he can mail them all in one official envelope. He wanted to take them back with him, but I told him I wanted to bring them and show them to a trusted friend first. They don't have to know it was you."

"Wouldn't the Commission be shocked if they found I can read those documents?" Molly said, picking up the envelope on the kitchen table holding the three letters.

"I wish you wouldn't make light of it. You know they don't like it when they find out we can read and write for ourselves, especially a female. I found that out a long time ago. When I finally taught myself to be darn good at, I had to say I couldn't, in hopes they wouldn't take away what was already mine. People want to take everything when they think you are too uppity. But it seems pretending like I don't know how, doesn't always help out—the way I thought it would." Alex said.

"I don't see how much worse off we could get with them knowing I can read," Molly said, as she turned to put away the breakfast plates.

୶

Alex left early the next morning to see his attorney.

"Mr. Yancy, sir. May I take a look at the letter you wrote to introduce my case? I am praying that it goes through. My Molly has already told me that this is just about the last appeal she will put up with. You being a man know how the woman can be when she wants to put an end to something, and my Molly is a woman and a half.'"

"Yes—well, that's alright, sure Mr. Powell, I have it here in the yellow folder on the side of my desk. Your correct name's on it. I've already sent an introductory wire to save time, then I'll send this letter."

The lawyer picked up the folder and out slid two white documents; first a copy of the telegram, the second item addressed to the The Department of the Interior with his signature as Alex's counsel at the bottom of the second sheet along with Alex's.

A written acknowledgement of the telegram and formal letter was received two weeks later, before he would dare to mention this most recent attempt to his wife again.

Attorney urges the Commission to grant Powells entitled rights

Muskogee, Ind. Ter., February 3, 1907.

Commissioner of Indian Affairs,

Washington, D. C.

As attorney for Alexander Philip Powell and fifteen children, applicants identification Mississippi Choctaws, in view early expiration Department's jurisdiction, earnestly urge immediate consideration application to reopen filed a year ago. These people are undoubtedly entitled to enrollment and want opportunity to offer evidence, and are now here ready to go before Commissioner Bixby. Applicants family is numerous and hence property rights involved are of great value. Respectfully request that motion be granted and Commissioner Bixby be notified by wire at once so that evidence may be taken and transmitted for decision within time limit. Copy hereof is being filed with Commissioner Bixby. Kindly wire answer.

David W. Yancey.

(Copy of Telegram.)

Yancy Files Petition for Rehearing, Feb 18, 1907

BEFORE THE DEPARTMENT OF THE INTERIOR.

(Through the Commissioner to the Five Civilized Tribes)

In the Matter of the Application of A. P. Powell and 15 children for Identification as Mississippi Choctaws.	MCR-1625. PETITION FOR REHEARING.

Comes now the above named applicant, and for himself and on behalf of his fifteen children, respectfully prays that this case be reopened and the Commissioner to the Five Civilized Tribes be authorized to take the additional testimony which has been discovered since the last hearing herein, and petitioner respectfully shows that if a rehearing is allowed he can prove that he is the son of Alexander Wilmer and Fannie Potubbee; that said Alexander Wilmer was the son of Tukelubbee and Susan Wilmer; that the said Fannie Potubbee was the daughter of Potubbee and Susan Buckner; that the said Potubbee was the son of one Oklahomah or Osletonot; that the said Oklahomah, Tukelubbee, Susan Wilmer, Alexander Wilmer, and Potubbee were all full blood Choctaw Indians; that the said Susan Buckner was a Portugese woman, and not of Indian blood; that the said Fannie Potubbee was one-half blood Choctaw; that the said Tukelubbee, Oklahomah, and Potubbee were beneficiaries under the Treaty of 1830.

Petitioner further respectfully shows that at the time he testified before the Commission to the Five Civilized Tribes on

(2)

the previous hearing of this case he was misinformed as to who his ancestors were, and that hence said record is in error in some respects; that since said hearing he has made further investigation with the result that he will now be able to prove that he and his fifteen children are entitled to be identified as Mississippi Choctaws.

Petitioner files herewith the affidavits of himself and of Joe Jamison and Martha Jamison, and respectfully prays that his said case be reopened and that he be allowed to introduce the additional evidence which he has discovered since the former hearing hereof, and he will ever pray.

Muskogee, Indian Territory, February 18, 1907.

For himself and fifteen children.

By _____

Muskogee, Indian Territory,
Counsel for Applicants.

PART V

26

PURVEYORS OF JUSTICE VS. THE FAMILY

IT HAD BEEN five years since the Powells were forced to come to Oklahoma. Unlike Mississippi, farms didn't produce as well, and houses were sprinkled here and there with the smell of cattle and open spaces replacing pine trees, rivers and green wooded areas. There were times when brutal winds and rolling storms forced them to open their windows to keep the room from bursting open from the pressure. Now, without notice, since Oklahoma had achieved statehood, Indian Territory had been extinguished, and the Powell family would be forced to pay rent on a tiny piece of land further north.

In some towns, blacks lived free from the prejudices and brutality found in other racially mixed communities of the Midwest and the South. Blacks in Oklahoma and Indian Territories would create their own communities for many reasons. Escape from discrimination and abuse would be a driving factor. All-Black settlements offered the advantage of being able to depend on neighbors for financial assistance and of having open markets for crops.

All-Black towns grew in Indian Territory after the Civil War, when the former slaves of the Five Tribes settled together for mutual protection and economic security. When the United States government forced American Indians to accept individual land allotments, most Indian "freedmen" chose land next to other blacks. They created cohesive, prosperous farming communities that could support businesses, schools, and churches, eventually forming towns. Entrepreneurs in these communities started every imaginable kind of business, including newspapers, and advertised throughout the South for settlers.

Many blacks migrated to Oklahoma, considering it a kind of Promised Land.

However, in some areas, the rough landscape and thin soils, lumbering, and grazing made only a minimal amount of farming possible. Alex and his family survived the earlier dry spells that lasted for weeks at a time, which created mounds of dust. As it tumbled through his fingers, the dry gritty earth took some time to get used to.

Alex vowed to get his rightful inheritance, and whatever the cost, he would keep his family together for the time being. Soon, the oldest children, who had been indispensable to them, would be on their own, trying to find their place in what had proven to be a harsh world—which sought to claim their father's pride and dignity.

Alex and Molly now had 15 living children. They lost one son to illness. Years earlier, before they married, Alex was 20 when he finally learned what Molly referred to as *proper talking*. She always believed he talked the other way with her just to annoy her and be playful. All those "gits", "em's", and "shucks" when they were youngsters. By the time they'd married, Alex had been proficient enough in speaking that he was respected as a teacher by the townspeople; just like they did Molly. His ability to speak well, though, didn't change the fact that Alex had to farm to keep up his share of the family support. Seeing that they both were considered mulattos, in the early years, they were able to survive in places with blacks and whites, but they were never totally accepted by either. Outside of Indian Territory, it seemed the only designations for people were either black or white. There was no in-between.

In the past, Alex had done all he could as an educated member of the tribe, by going time after time to the Dawes Commission, and not judging any man according to some government classification. A year earlier, Alex believed he'd finally swayed the acting commissioner in his favor when the official told him to, "Go out and select all the land for yourself and your children. We will set it aside, and we will allow you to rent it and lease it out, but we won't give you any certificate."

All members of the Commission on Indian Affairs knew Alexander/Anthony/A.P. Powell by either of the three names and had compiled over 100 pages of his depositions and appeals in their files—more than any other applicant since its inception. He couldn't believe they balked at him in one letter for doing what he was instructed to do by their commissioner—it was to pick out the piece of land he would like if he moved to Indian Territory in Oklahoma.

Alex selected 2,500 acres of land for his family. At the close of the rolls, he had a farm where he made 42 bales of cotton on it; and 2,000 bushels of corn, and a house–not some tumble-down shack, and they took it all from him.

By this time, the self-proclaimed purveyors of America's "truth and justice" had grown weary of Mr. Powell and his determination. He was denied his appeals each and every year, without the benefit of explanation or a second thought.

Molly slid open the door and slipped into the room. She picked up the crumbled letter at Alex's feet, he'd picked up at the post that morning, and read it.

MCR-1625.

Muskogee, Indian Territory, February 14, 1907.

Anthony P. Powell,
    C/o Robt. E. Lee,
        Ardmore, Indian Territory.

Dear Sir:-

      You are hereby notified that on February 6, 1907, the Secretary of the Interior denied a motion, filed May 23, 1906, by Robt. E. Lee, attorney at law, Ardmore, Indian Territory, for a rehearing in the Mississippi Choctaw case of Anthony P. Powell et al.

                Respectfully,

                               Commissioner.

So, while the Powell children were outside tossing a ball under clear blue skies, their father was inside unraveling. Alex could not believe God would allow the Commission to withhold what he deserved; what was handed down to him from his grandfather and father. To Alex—it felt like he was being reprimanded for fighting for his dignity and land. *It belonged to him.* His attorney agreed. Was the Commission's rejection all because he pointed out the land he would like to receive in the Oklahoma Indian territory? Something which *they* had instructed Alex to do.

For the sake of his children, whom he watched playing outside from his bedroom window, Alex would never stop appealing. His spirit labeled this as the ultimate war between good and evil. He held his ground as sheriffs were instructed to order his family out of their present dwelling within the Oklahoma Indian Territory.

"They will have to kill me if they want me to stop fighting," he said loud enough for his wife to quiet him.

Molly begged him not to say those words. It was so unlike the man she loved. She couldn't lose him to this fight over land.

27
LOVE PREVAILS

U NABLE TO STAND the strain anymore, Molly broke down when their lawyer told them everything he learned of the lengthy ruling from the Commission. Attorney Yancy had to dig to get this information, as they never gave an actual explanation, only a short statement of rejection. Now holding the letter in her trembling hands, she read that the Commission was not satisfied with Alex's witnesses, affidavits and depositions. The significance of every word on the pages glared at her. How could they believe her Alex was anything but a man of integrity? She didn't understand which ancestor they were questioning here.

Indian Commission Cites Conflicting Evidence

J. W. G.

J. C. H.

(C O P Y)

DEPARTMENT OF THE INTERIOR,

WASHINGTON.

I. T. D.448-1907.   February 6, 1907.
D. C.7793.

L. R. S.

The Commissioner to the Five Civilized Tribes,

Muskogee, Indian Territory.

Sir:-

May 26, 1906, you transmitted a petition for rehearing
in the matter of the application of Anthony P. Powell, et al.
for identification as Mississippi Choctaws. On May 21, 1902,
the Department affirmed the decision of the Commission to the
Five Civilized Tribes, dated April 15, 1902, adverse to all the
claimants. November 16, 1903 (I. T. D.9271-1903), a motion for
rehearing of the case wasdenied by the Department and on
January 30, 1905 (I. T. D.7716, 12530-1904), a further motion
to have the application considered as one for enrolment by
blood was also denied.

Reporting January 8, 1907, the Indian Office (Land 81661-
1906), recommended that the present motion be denied. Copy of
its letter is inclosed.

The principal applicant originally claimed descent from
Tuk-e-lubbee, a full blood, through applicant's father,
Alexander Wilmer. Applicant swore on his examination before
the Commission in Mississippi in April, 1901, that his mother

-2-

was a colored woman, a slave, and that he took his name, Powell,
from her rather than the name of his father, Wilmer, as it was
customary for children who were born in slavery to take the
name of the mother. He now claims that the stenographer who
reported his testimony before the Commission in 1901 made
numerous errors and that he did not say that his mother had
no Indian blood, but claimed that she was part Choctaw, and he
now further claims that she was the daughter of one Po-tubbee,
who was the son of Os-lot-o-not or Ok-loh-o-mah.

The testimony with reference to the blood of the applicant's mother, as originally reported, bears no evidence of
being an error as it rests not on a single question and answer
but on a series of questions and answers which entirely har-
monize, and was further corroborated by the affidavit of D. H.
Tindall, filed on June 24, 1901, in support of the original
record.

Isaac Johnson, in his affidavit filed in support of the
present motion, states "that he himself had seen Po-tubbee's
patent, a sheepskin writing," whereas the records of the Land
Office show that the Po-tubbee, who was the son of Ok-loh-o-mah,
received scrip which was transferred and used by William C.
Wilson, assignee, for taking land at Clarksville, Arkansas,
July 19, 1851, and the records of the Indian Office further
show that the identical Po-tubbee referred to arrived in the
Choctaw Nation west with his family, consisting of one man and
two women, on May 16, 1851. It is but fair to presume, in the

-3-

absence of evidence to the contrary, that they did not subse-
quently return to Mississippi, where the applicant's mother
lived and died, as is conclusively shown by the testimony. If a
return be admitted, it would still be unlikely that Po-tubbee's
daughter would have been subjected to slavery thereafter.

The evidence is also conflicting as to the names and places
of residence of the alleged ancestors. In the motion it is
claimed that Os-lot-o-net and Ok-loh-o-mah are the same person.
The Indian Office records show that Ok-loh-o-mah was a woman,
and affiant, Joe Jamison, states that Os-lot-o-not was the
father of Po-tubbee. Affiant, Isaac Johnson, states that he
lived in Jasper County, Mississippi, and knew a full-blood
named Po-tubbee, who lived and held land from the Government
in Kemper County, Mississippi. Affiant, Joe Jamison, further
states that he lived in Newton County, Mississippi, where he
knew the ancestor of A. P. Powell and that Po-tubbee's family
lived in the portion of Mississippi when affiant first knew
them where Kemper County now is. The Indian Office records
show that the ancestor, Oh-loh-o-mah, lived in Neshoba County,
Mississippi. It further appears that the principal applicant's
maternal grandmother was Susan Buckner or Susan Powell, but
there is no evidence of any kind to show that she was ever the
wife of Po-tubbex or even so much as acquainted with him.

In view of the conflicting evidence in the case and the
change in the line of ancestry through whom the applicants now
claim, the Department does not consider that a sufficient show-

-4-

ing has been made to warrant a rehearing and the motion is accordingly denied.

The record in the case has been sent to the Indian Office for its files.

Respectfully,

Thos Ryan,

First Assistant Secretary.

1 inc. & 20 to Ind. Of.

Through the Commissioner
of Indian Affairs.

While attempting to calm Molly, and also listen to what his lawyer had to say, Alex wrote down all he could for reference.

"They've twisted everything I said in this ruling of theirs... everything. I'm trying to remember it all, but I'm at my wits end that they will crucify a man, if they can, for not remembering exact details from almost 100 years ago... I wasn't even there!" he shouted. "They use their laws against me that they don't even follow—the way they want everyone else to do. First, they do this to Cioak, and he a full blood Choctaw, now it's my turn, 'cause I'm not Choctaw enough. My background is mixed with more than just the white man."

Later, it was Alex who needed comforting.

"What does all this mean, Molly? How am I supposed to remember every single ancestor, every percentage and every iota of everything back past before I was born? I remember the little I saw, the few people I knew, and what I was told by the old folks. I can't believe they ask anyone else all these questions, and put them through this inquisition for land their father owned, that they've been living on all their lives."

Lying on the bed covers next to him, Molly didn't interrupt her husband who needed to keep talking.

"I believe it pleases them to see us suffer, Molly. They know that there is so much land that belongs to others besides them, but they won't give up even a speck—just to be ornery. I thought things had changed, but it's no different. Look at our children. They believe in us. What do they have to look forward to? I've got to keep them believing in me—woman, don't you understand? Those men on the Commission want me to go away–all of us. But I'll die first."

That was it for Molly.

She couldn't stand to hear him talk this way. "Stop it, stop. I told you before to stop saying things like that to me.

Don't you talk about dying to me!"

His jaw held firm, despite seeing the tears welling up in his wife's still, beautiful eyes.

She cried, "What am I if you are not here to wrap your

arms around me night after night? I'm nothing if I lose you, Lord help me, forgive me for saying that, but it's true. Nothing, nothing at all!"

Alex softened his stance, grabbed his wife and pulled her underneath him. "It's no different for me, Molly. I need you.

"And, I will do whatever, say whatever, for my family to survive."

Alex leaned his slightly graying head to one side and held his wife tight—loving her, as always–no matter what.

In the still of the night, Molly worried whether Alex would really go so far as he threatened. She had never seen him like this before, and she hated the men on that Commission responsible for making him this way. This life was so hard with no help, she thought. It's even harder when the very ones who always help their own, do all they can to stop anyone who would try to help you and yours.

She vowed— as she'd roused her sleeping husband to offer herself over mind and body—that she would not let them take her man down this way.

28

HOLDING ON

MOLLY GOT UP the next morning and picked up where Alex left off the night before. She hadn't gotten a moment's rest.

"I won't let them do this to you? I do not believe they have traced back to 1820, going through records that they say they have, simply because they suspect the percentage you claim of Choctaw blood is a little off. How do they believe you've owned that land, all these years? They even have down on that last census that you owned it. But they've just pushed us off, so they can give it to someone else."

Molly couldn't seem to stop herself. "Then they try to claim some land was procured on your mother's father Potubbe's side and sold to a third party. In the same breath, they attempt to state your mother is not Potubbe's child, because she happened to be mixed with Negro blood."

"And they're all gone now," Alex murmured, thinking of how fleeting life really was.

"Where'd they go?" One of the younger boys asked, who'd just come in from outside.

"Shhh." Molly dreaded having to explain death to the

youngest children, although she'd lost one child. Despite what she'd felt about the hereafter, based on what Ma had taught her, she still hadn't discussed it, not just yet with the younger ones. Hurriedly, she shot up from her winged back chair and placed two bowls of hot grits in the middle of the long wooden kitchen table, motioning for Alex to drop down onto the cane stool next to the boy.

Molly reverted to memories of Ma, while Alex drew strength from his father, and both tried hard not to sound bitter. They reached across the table and grasped hands in silent agreement that the Lord would provide.

Molly looked up from bending over to help their youngest son into his short trousers. Seeing her man's penetrating gaze—she knew she was loved.

Still feeling the warmth of his adoration, she returned her attention to the struggling little one—telling him to try to smile in spite of the upcoming move.

"Ma, why do I gotta look happy when I ain't?" he asked. "Fine—boy," she said. Considering the situation, she let him be—for questioning her and using the word "ain't.

๙

After having settled in Carter County, in the tiny town of Homer near Ardmore for over six years, the family was forced to move further north to Nowata, a city with over 3000 people. The town was situated in northeastern Oklahoma, and served as the county seat for Nowata County, an area sprinkled with mountain ranges, summits and mountain gaps. The land also included woodland belts, limestone and sandstone hills, limestone quarries and shallow oil fields.

Years earlier, Alex had appealed the courts original decision of 1902 and 1903, stating they "found Tukeelubee of the same name as Alex's grandfather to be a boy of three, instead of an adult male." Not only was Alex not sure that they found a boy of three with the same name, but if they did—it didn't matter. He knew the man who came to visit them as a child, gave him that pony, had identified himself as his grandfather. His name he said was the same name—Tukeelubee. This was Tukeelubee and his people's land, and Alex knew now he was up against a fight, the same as his grandfather, with those who were determined to take it away from him.

"Hold on to Ma's joy, even when there seems so little reason to…" Molly smiled, mouthing the sentiment for her husband's sake more than feeling it.

"I know, baby. I know." Alex said squeezing her fingers tighter.

❧

In 1908, after Yancy's appeal failed, Alex and Molly had another baby, a little boy they nicknamed A.C. In order to keep her family together, in spite of the possibility of a new life without her husband's rightful inheritance, Molly got down on her knees every night along with her strong, fearless man and prayed to the only God she knew—that he would hear their pleas for help.

Except there was the one time Molly couldn't bear to see the strain on her man's face any longer and errantly suggested, "We should just burst right into their offices and tell them how we know they give land away to whites, without them barely asking, much less having to prove themselves. I know some of those people were our friends, but it wasn't right how they just gave them the land and put us through this."

"Baby, you know a hot-tempered person stirs up conflict, but the one who is patient calms a quarrel," Alex reminded her of what they heard from the pastor in church service that past Sunday.

"I know, Alex, but maybe we need to have more *temper* and some more *conflict*, cause others are way too *calm* about trying to keep us in bondage."

Molly was afraid that her husband couldn't take another appeal, much less a rejection. This was his last hope. Her last hope. Her family's last hope.

Almost as if he read her thoughts, Alex offered comfort, "With us there will always be hope, with or without what has been wrenched from our grasp."

He suppressed his thoughts as he watched Molly move away to get the baby settled in his basket. He wouldn't let her see his fear and desperation... his eyes had lines in the corners that weren't there before. The gray strands on his head were coming faster than the seasons. He was on a mission to survive. He knew how fiery his wife's spirit was, and he wasn't going to let anyone hurt her because she was so fearless, and would take on anyone. He couldn't share his feelings with his still lovely bride—'cause that's what she'd always be to him—but if he failed this time, he didn't know how he could live this way.

Molly caught Alex's anguished expression out of the corner of her eye. Not wanting to bring him down any further, she called over to him, "It's gonna be fine and so will you! This family will go on no matter what... our children will continue to believe and be strong in the might of our Lord. That is what I believe. I have to. Ma would have it that way."

Molly strolled over to the bed they shared and lifted her husband's chin with her fingertips, "Come baby, let's rest now."

29

STRANGE MEMORIES

B EFORE RISING, ALEX lay in bed, his view blocked by the window covering with only a tiny triangular opening less than an inch in diameter where the sun peeked through.

Hundreds of tiny, bright parallel rays bounced off his irises, blinding him with its power and brilliance.

Staring into the glittering light, he vividly recalled an evening a few years earlier when his confidant, friend and now deceased neighbor Ed Carter came barreling through the front door like a freight train jumping the tracks, loosening a cobweb wedged in the upper corner of the frame.

Earlier that day, Alex had sent a note over by his boy, asking Mr. Carter to come by so they could discuss the strange men their neighbor Pettis said asked him and others to sign curious papers. Alex wished Carter had sobered up a bit before dropping in near evening when Molly and the children were around.

"Carter, being a notary and all, you've got a keen eye for when something's not right 'round here. That's why I called you over."

"Not me. "You're the fella who somehow seems to find out everything that's going on around here (hiccup). How's that?"

"I don't know. You have to keep your eyes and ears open, but sometimes it comes too late. Personally, I just pray to God that he will listen and understand, and I try to look out for my fellow man."

The oddly, inebriated man stumbled into the chair next to Alex, as he spoke, then roared loud enough for everyone who was not in the room to hear.

"You know there's some, especially the ornery ones, who don't trust the smiling types," he said. Maybe they got it right. They say if you are as ornery as they are, and hate-talk up a storm about somebody like them—then you *can* be trusted…" Alex questioned what the man sputtered forth, noting the disturbing manner in which his obviously, drunken friend burst in and fell into the seat next to him. He almost tipped it over.

The uninhibited neighbor wasn't done talking, "I don't know, but I think, uh, maybe you be wrong in believing you can be of help to everyone, yep, and most of all that you could trust anyone 'round here!"

"What do you mean?" Alex asked, trying to be kind.

"Maybe you just ain't seeing what's there." Carter said.

"Aren't you more than a little bit out of your gourd with drink, my friend?" Alex said, pointing at his very own right temple to imply what he meant.

"So, you 'spect I'm loaded… batty?! You think I'm out–"

"*THUMP!*"

"BANG!"

The man stopped in mid-stream, as both men leapt to opposite sides of the room at the jarring, loud noise outside, just before a strong gust hurled the front door open.

"Carter, did you push the door all the way closed when you came in?" Alex asked, pushing it close, after an icy breeze whipped around the room's interior, blowing papers from his desk, and knocking over the tin cup sitting on the wood- carved side table.

"Maybe–" Carter gulped, "too much wind and too much trusting folks, I say."

Alex mumbled something, while picking up his papers and the tin cup, and then asked of Carter, "What'd you say?"

"Pay me no mind (hiccup)," he said, poking around the room, then covering his mouth with a dusty hand.

Alex stepped away and checked outside the door, hoping Molly had tiptoed out back.

"Well, I 'spect the wind is always raw and fierce 'round this time of year," his friend said, sounding surprisingly coherent.

Then the man went on to challenge Alex's murmurings, which he thought no one heard.

"And about you thinking I'm wrong in saying you can't trust no one, well… jumpy as a young grasshopper, ain't you? Now you settle down and have a seat in yo' own place. I've got a lot more to tell you about this here tom foolery that's been happenin' round here (hiccup). I 'spect that's why you called me over, ain't it?"

After Carter left, Molly had said she didn't have to hold her tongue any longer about what she'd seen in her own house. "I know he's been a genuine friend, but why does he have to drink so much these days?" Molly asked, poking her head back into the room from around the kitchen.

Alex shrugged, and didn't answer her until later that night, when they were in bed.

"It's the only way he can tolerate all the happenings in his life." he said, then added, "It's only at night… not daytime."

"What kind of reason is that? He should just bear it, like the rest of us do." Molly said without thinking.

"You know some can't. Anyway, he refers to his drinking as consoling himself."

"Well, I just hate that the children have to see or hear. I don't like him near them when he's like that. I wish you'd find someone else to be friends with when he's that way."

"You know, I don't either, and his condition makes it hard to believe the things he says, but he's a smart fellow who wants to help. He didn't drink, you know that, before his wife passed on. He just can't handle as much without something strong to hold him these days."

Thoughts of a man losing his wife was something Alex didn't want to entertain. He reached up and cupped the side of Molly's face in his calloused hand. Then he pressed his lips to hers for a long moment, before laying down to rest. He had to be up early and ready for the day to come.

"What things?"

"Huh?"

"What things was he saying?" Molly asked, having heard some of it, but wanting to hear it again from her husband.

"Oh… nothing you'd want to know, though he was so sure of what he said, I think I'll to talk to our attorney about it. "Anyway," Alex reminded her. "You saw how he was.

"Let's get some rest, baby. Goodnight."

Before she returned his kiss, Molly said, "And even if he was sure of himself doesn't mean his story is worth looking into, either. Remember that! Good night, love."

It's hard to believe that was over three years ago, Alex said to himself, shaking his head at all that had happened since then, knowing he would again have to revisit the disturbing story surrounding what occurred that year.

30

REVELATIONS COME TO LIGHT

THE NEXT MORNING Molly rose up and examined herself in the looking glass. She'd aged quite a few years—she believed, but still felt nearly as attractive as that young girl she used to be. In her life, these days, there was no time for a lot of primping with the "quagmire full of duties" pressed upon a struggling farmer's wife—with children. Once in a while, her thoughts lingered on what her life would have been like if she'd stayed in Boston all those years ago. But she quickly shrugged off that thought, when she pictured herself having to wrestle with her face every day to get it into high society form. No need for that here, she smiled, still satisfied with her choice.

Eveline, her oldest girl, entered the room to find her mother grinning at herself in the looking glass. In her reflection, Molly could see her daughter who came in from the kitchen after preparing breakfast for her younger sisters and brothers.

"I don't know," Molly laughed. "Gravity is doing its best to haul this face to the ground."

"Oh mother, you're still playing teacher with that 'gravity' talk," Eveline laughed, "Anyway, you're still very pretty, no matter what. Oh, now I remember why I came in. I've been thinking about maybe going to a teacher's college somewhere, if I could. What do you think?"

"I think it's wonderful, my dear."

Grateful for such a daughter, Molly thought, it was *her* time now… to be free and happy. Molly wished she and Alex could have given her more time to do what she wished, but they always needed her so much. Molly wanted to gift her with those special lotions she'd heard about from up North to help with those scaly, dry patches behind her knees and elbows. Molly couldn't forget her own affliction of youth, when her foot would drag on the ground if she became overwrought. She only experienced two or three bouts over recent years, when she became completely exhausted from the strain of having babies barely a year apart. She remembered some of the ladies from the church had come to help out.

Molly recalled those years they attended Blackjack Missionary Baptist Church with Ma, particularly one Sunday when a churchgoer prophesied over Alex. Their entire crew walked in about five minutes after the service had already started and tiptoed to their row. Ten ladies and four men were leading the congregation in "Nearer My God to Thee" from the choir loft in front of the small brown and white church. The pastor began praying for the Lord to intervene for all whom their forefathers had called on and who they now trust for their guidance. That's when an elderly woman she'd seen once before raised up from her seat in the front bench pew and hobbled down the middle aisle. She stopped right next to the spot where Alex was seated at the end of the row where they sat near the back. The woman's eyes closed as a hush fell throughout the sanctuary which had been preceded by whispering and "shushes".

"Folks that thinks and feels much," she had proclaimed, "be the best judge of the inner spirits of those around them. There's some things only they can see… some unwritten revelation… protect thyself."

Molly emerged from her thoughts at the sound of Alex's familiar voice. She looked around the room, noting that Eveline had long gone, having left her mother alone with her thoughts.

"Molly, Moll! Baby, I know we put off talking about this, but I've decided to make that trip to Washington. There's no other way," Alex said. "We've been fighting nine years of our lives and they want me to give up, but I won't. I know there are others depending on me now, besides our family. If they can do this to me, how many other men like me do you think they've done this to. I'm not losing hope."

"Alex, I'm scared," she said, trying to shake off the memory she just had. "Do you have to go all the way to Washington, D.C? I know people are different there, but now I'm not so sure if they are as different as I once believed them to be years ago when I was in Boston."

"What else can we do? I've tried and tried, over and over again. I've got respectable folks of every race and color who have vouched for me. I offered them the documents they ask me for year after year, but now because people write things down wrong, they say to my lawyers, I'm no-count. They won't give a man like me the benefit of the doubt. I keep going back to that wrong name on their census when we were first married. They aren't saying it, but could that be why they don't trust me? I know it can't be the first time one of those enumerators got someone's name down different from one ten-year period to the next in that census of theirs. Are they trying to use that mistake of theirs—the man said didn't matter—against us? We feared something worse could've happened if we challenged their errors on the census. Maybe I shouldn't have let them leave it like that in the last one, if that *is* one of their reasons. I know who I am. No matter now... but I don't know how else I can prove my grandfather's name should be on the Choctaw rolls. That's what I was told. Now they say it's not there –his name, Tukeelubee."

Molly moved to get up, but sat back down when Alex reached for her.

"I plan to tell them everything, Moll. Even the part they never wanted to hear. I have everything to lose or win now."

"How those men came and lied about you to get you from speaking and helping the others?" Molly asked.

He nodded.

"It's obvious these men from the Commission don't want to hear that, Alex, not if it will help you or us. But those men in Washington D.C. are not southern men, but gentlemen from up North, so maybe they will think different, act better."

She paused.

"Although at times," Molly added, "I worry that it won't matter all that much. They may show you better treatment—the rest remains to be seen."

Both rose and took turns removing the breakfast dishes from the table, placing them in the large pan in the sink for washing.

"Well, I mean to tell them what Pettis and Franklin did by going to my neighbors to slander my name, even after I tried to help them to read and write so they could learn to stand up for themselves. And that's just one of the low-down dirty tactics they use around here. I know not everyone I thought was my friend is behind me. Some have a wide smile which doesn't equal a pure heart. Maybe that's where I went wrong, believing that those that smile the hardest at me are the ones who are behind me. Old Joe smiles and says something nice every time I see him. He's our friend, right? Wrong. I believe that the same tactics were used when my mother wasn't allowed to get on the Choctaw rolls by that Commissioner Ward. My people took the wrong side in the war as far as they were concerned and tried to help the wrong people in their eyes, but those were the ones we trusted, based off their countenance, maybe we should have dug a little deeper to find the truth."

With every word he spoke, Alex began to believe more and more of the things Carter had told to him, but he knew he would have to do a lot of digging to prove it.

"Molly, one day soon, I will tell them all. And I won't have to litter my conversation with yes'm and yas sirs like I had to in

Meridian to get them to listen to me. Your husband will speak as the educated man that he is, and will no longer have to bow down, in hopes of pleasing men who would only be pleased by my poverty and degradation.

"We will stand in Washington. We will stand." He promised.

Molly grasped her husband's hand between her soapy fingers, letting him know that she was always with him—no matter what—they were united.

Alex dried her hands with the cloth and pulled her close. "My *pretty one*," he said, borrowing her nickname from the past.

31

LOST THOUGHTS AND
OTHER THINGS

IN 1909, DESPITE wading through a rain drenched
November, that year and the next were the onset of one of
the driest spells in Oklahoma's history.

It was at the start of that next year that Molly had received
crushing news that hit her harder than most anyone would
understand. As if the current strain of her husband and family
wasn't difficult enough, only Ma who had passed on herself,
and Alex and her children would understand.

Although she suspected others in Grenada also knew, she'd
never tell anyone outside her family–only her children, and
they would tell their children one day.

Walter Neuman (H.Tindall)—one of the most thoroughgoing men in Mississippi, her childhood benefactor—her father
had passed away. It had been more than 15 years since his life
story was published in the *Historical and Biographical Memoirs
of Mississippi's Most Worthy and Illustrious Families/Individuals.*

Molly wondered if he ever told anyone about her, like
she'd told her husband and children, that she was his own. In
any case, Molly knew why he probably hadn't, he and Ma had

promised each other they wouldn't reveal their secret. Molly wondered if Mississippi's highfalutin' society would have published all those wonderful—and yes, true–things about him if they knew about he and Ma and their child.

His last act of kindness to Molly could have jeopardized his privacy, she thought. He did everything he could to help her and Alex secure their land; providing affidavits to the Commission on Indian Affairs, offering up his reputation to solidify the truth—that he was well acquainted with Alex's Choctaw father. Short of giving her an inheritance—which went to his wife and his children in marriage–Molly concluded that he'd proved that he loved her and Ma by his limited, but meaningful, words and actions to help her family.

Yet, with all of this man's honorable intentions and those of countless others who knew Alex's father, it wasn't enough for the Commission to do right by him, his wife and children.

◈

Molly's concerns about Alex had surpassed worry.

On his birthday, Alex had always remembered the day he was born, maybe not the exact year all the time. It was in May he always said. Yet for the last two years, he hadn't mentioned it once, and Molly was afraid to bring it up. She'd wondered if he had forgotten or had begun to despise his life—that day he came into existence. He was misplacing and forgetting other things too, even the children at one point, and laughed about it when she told him.

"I'm fine baby," he said, "I'll get back to my senses when all this is done."

With his whole existence aimed at getting back what belonged to him, Molly couldn't help thinking of his cousin Cioak, and how he became twisted with bitterness over his stolen inheritance. She couldn't shake the image of how they found him that day so long ago, bloody and lifeless against a tree in the deep woods; so much so, she screamed aloud before she quickly clutched her hand over her mouth.

PART VI

32

THE MAN FROM MISSOURI

A FTER YEARS OF going back and forth with various attorneys and law firms, fending off inquiries of the Powell family and their neighbors by suspicious strangers, and traveling back to Mississippi to obtain critical documents from libraries and courthouses; it was now two weeks before Alex would leave for Washington D.C. to plead his case before the Representatives of U.S. Congress. He had prepared for this day not only for the last three years; but all of his life. He spoke for his family, those who came before him, his descendants, and every man who like him would have to survive on this earth in the years to come.

He'd memorized a portion of the statement he'd prepared and within it he had every intention of letting these Federal men in Washington know what he'd found.

Praying the strain would begin to lessen, once he could finally reveal all that he'd learned, Alex's concentration obscured his vision. He discounted the magnificence of the Capitol building and its expansive green lawns, beautiful trees, and artwork which lined the walls as he was directed to the south wing where the House members met.

It was the morning of April 2, 1910. Alex took his place behind another gentleman who was looking around the room, while wiping his forehead with a slightly, worn gray handkerchief. Alex assumed he also wished to give testimony before Congress. Both were preceded by an attorney, whom Alex learned was from St. Louis, Missouri. He didn't know the distinguished gentleman, but in listening to him, while waiting outside to speak, Alex knew this man understood everything he and Molly and those like them had endured. The truthful, urgent appeal of H. J. Cantwell brought Alex to tears such that he had to pull out his own handkerchief to mop his eyes and then his brow:

> "… It is absolutely imperative, however, that this committee determine, and determine speedily, the questions of law. The committee will do more to finally settle the affairs of this tribe by careful consideration of the laws already passed, by which they will be convinced that the purpose of the general legislation has been subverted by cunning distortion of a word here and there; and a few simple enactments to correct these errors and distortions under which new enactment the Department of the Interior may go ahead and determine facts expeditiously, will do more to solve the complicated problem than if Congress should create a dozen courts or a dozen commissions to hear facts.

> I submit the intent of the treaty and the plain intent of Congress has been subverted by legislation. The subversion must be corrected by legislation. I am inclined to believe, after a careful study of the testimony taken before the respective committees that the Dawes Commission, or any member of it, was not guilty of

fraud. The injustice and inequalities here complained of is the result of a misconception of the powers and the rights of the purely ornamental tribal organizations and of the mistaken notion which the Indians have conceived that this domain is a matter of their private inheritance, and that while they shall individually themselves receive the proceeds of all the lands, with the great increase thereto which civilization has given, on the theory that they are the living successors of the persons once composing a political community, they deny that right to others who have equal claims in law and in nature to the same benefit.

Add to this consideration, moving a large number of people, the spirit of intolerance against a race formerly held in slavery, and the baleful results followed naturally and inevitably, unless the superintending power of the United States had been constantly and intelligently manifested.

Justice, gentlemen, has been long absent from her throne in the Indian country where the right of a "nigger" was in any way involved. Intolerance, ignorance, error, and perhaps, sometimes, fraud, has usurped and occupied her place. We humbly pray that the blind goddess who weighs true with her scales the claims of white, of Indian, of white-Indian, of Indian-negro, and negro-Indian, shall now be restored to her judgment seat, and that her reign, so auspiciously begun in 1893, and which continued uninterruptedly until 1898, shall again prevail."

H. J. Cantwell.

[Actual Documentation]

Alex wondered if this attorney Cantwell could somehow

be acquainted with the lawyer who'd helped Molly's brother years ago. He remembered the story she recounted to him of Henry Lawson and how her brother would have never made his way back from Memphis to Grenada alive if it wasn't for the man's benevolence.

As the questioning legislator's names were being announced, Alex was now being summoned to enter the speaking area.

33

ONE OF THREE INDIANS

ALEX TOOK HIS place on the imposing Senate floor.
His time had finally come to tell his story to those who
would listen. He vowed that he would not leave until
these honorable men see and hear, firsthand, the man that he
was...

Actual Documentation: Narration [in brackets]

The documented house congressional speakers ques-
tioning Alex (Phillips Powell) were: The Chairman Chas
A. Burke, S. Dakota; John H. Stephens, Texas; Richard
A. Ballinger, U.S. Secretary of the Interior; Bird Mc
Guire, OK; N. E. Kendall, Iowa; Arthur P. Murphy,
Virginia; E. P. Hill, Attorney for Choctaw Nation.

STATEMENT OF ALEXANDER PHILLIPS POWELL, A
MISSISSIPPI CHOCTAW INDIAN.
April 2, 1910.

The Chairman: There were two or three Indians here who, it was suggested, ought to have five minutes a piece, and I thought if we could hear two or three of them we could relieve them, as I understand they have been waiting here some time.

Now, Mr. Stephens, you may present the Indians.

Mr. Stephens: Mr. Powell has asked to be heard. He is a Mississippi Choctaw.

The Chairman: How many are there of them?

Mr. Stephens: Only two; Mr. Powell and [another man who wishes to speak].

The Chairman: Now, Mr. Powell, you can make your statement.

Mr. Powell: Mr. Chairman, I can explain what I have to say in four or five minutes. In the first place, I am a Mississippi Choctaw who came under the terms of the fourteenth article of the treaty of 1830, the treaty made on September 27, 1830, at Dancing Rabbit Creek. I am the son of a Mississippi Choctaw, if the records are correct; the son of Alexander Wilmer, who was a full-blood Choctaw Indian. His father was named Tukelubbe, who was a full-blood Choctaw Indian, in compliance with the nineteenth article of the treaty of 1830, if the records are right.

Mr. Ballinger: Show them where your grandfather's name appears on the record or rolls there.

Mr. Powell: Grandpapa Tukelubbe's name appears in volume 7, page 73, of the American State Papers.

Mr. Stephens: Did you ever get any land from the United States Government on land scrip—your grandfather's

Mr. Powell: Yes, sir.

Mr. Stephens: On which side, or both?

Mr. Powell: Both applied. One applied under the terms of the nineteenth article of the treaty of 1830; Grandpapa Tukelubbe did.

Mr. Stephens: What did the other comply with?

Mr. Powell: He took land in Mississippi. He got a scrip, 272 B. I would like to introduce that scrip. I nave it with me.

Mr. Stephens: Go on and explain what you have done; what you have done to get on the roll.

Mr. Kendall: You say you took Scrip 272 B?

Mr. Powell: That is, Grandpapa Tukelubbe, on my mother's side.[transcripts should state: Pottubbe]

Mr. Stephens: Tell where you went, and for what purpose?

Mr. Powell: This man was the son of Oklahoma.

Mr. Kendall: Did you remove from Mississippi up to Oklahoma?

Mr. Powell: Yes.

In the next place, the Dawes Commission came to Mississippi in 1901 for the purpose of identifying the Mississippi Choctaws that failed to go West when the other Choctaws emigrated, and they told us that we had to leave Mississippi and go West in the Indian Territory, which was provided for under the terms of the fourteenth article of the treaty of 1830.

Up to that time we had decided to settle in Mississippi, and remain in the land once owned by our forefathers. Being a tribe of Indians, never in the history of time were we guilty of raising arm against a white man. We were always loyal to our country and Government. We held meetings and thought it best to yield to the wishes of the Dawes Commission. We were then shipped out from Mississippi by speculators as you would treat cattle. When we got to the Indian Territory hundreds of our people were denied their rights in a land among injurious strangers, thousands of miles from our eastern home, dependent, and without anything to go on. I have often thought and said to my people in holding meetings that any fair-minded Congressman would be for the Mississippi Choctaws if he knew the real facts of the case. Many of those people died, I claim, from grief in the Indian Territory, more recently Oklahoma, from the way they were treated.

I appeal to the Committee on Indian Affairs to give us a showing, and to enact some legislation whereby we may be given our share of allotments of land in the Choctaw and Chickasaw nations, more recently Oklahoma.

> *Mr. Stephens:* Would the bill I have introduced for you accomplish that purpose? It recites that all Mississippi Choctaw Indians whose fathers or grandparents had received lands from the United States Government and had removed to the Indian Territory in the time required by law should be permitted now to have their cases examined by the Secretary of the Interior, and if found to be Choctaw Indians, that they should be enrolled, and should receive their part of the land and property coming to the Indians. You have read the bill, have you not?

> *Mr. Powell:* Yes. That would save, Mr. Stephens, one of us out of ten, maybe.

> *Mr. Stephens:* How many individuals would that put on the roll? Mr. Powell. Of the Mississippi Choctaws it would not put on over 150. I think you will agree with me.

> *The Chairman:* How many went to Oklahoma?

> *Mr. Powell:* About 5,000.

> *The Chairman:* How many of those were enrolled?

Mr. Powell: There were fully 2,000 left off under the terms of the fourteenth article of the treaty of 1830.

The Chairman: Did you go there at that time?

Mr. Powell: Yes, sir.

The Chairman: And were you denied enrollment?

Mr. Powell: I had to appear under the terms of the fourteenth article, being three-quarters Indian and one-quarter Portuguese, and I had to go back and link on to an ancestor under the fourteenth article. The full blood had no answer to make.

Mr. McGuire: You are one-quarter Portuguese?

Mr. Powell: Yes, sir. That puts me under the fourteenth article.

The Chairman: Where do you live now?

Mr. Powell: In the Indian Territory.

The Chairman: Are there any Mississippi Choctaws still in Mississippi?

Mr. Powell: Yes. A few went back. Some of them walked back.

The Chairman: You say this bill of Mr. Stephens would affect about 150?

Mr. Powell: It would not put on over 150, because it has been eighty years since the treaty of Dancing Rabbit Creek was made, and we would have to link on to evidence, and the living witnesses, supposing they were 15 years old at that time, most assuredly would have to be 95 years old, and you gentlemen know they are not living.

Mr. Stephens: Have you land of your own that you were put on down there in Oklahoma farms that you were cultivating?

Mr. Powell: I, being an educated member of the tribe, kept going to the Dawes Commission time after time, and I finally convinced Fred Marr and Acting Commissioner William O. Beall, and finally they said, "Go out and select all the land for yourself and your children and we will set it aside, and we will allow you to rent it and lease it out, but we won't give you any certificate."

I selected 2,500 acres of land for myself and my children. At the close of the rolls I had a farm where I made 42 bales of cotton on it; that was in 1907; and 2,000 bushels of corn, and I had a house, and they have taken all that from me.

The Chairman: You did have the land, and when the rolls were closed you were stricken from the roll and lost your property?

Mr. Powell: Yes.

Mr. [McGuire]: Where did you go to school?

Mr. Powell: In Mississippi.

Mr. McGuire: In the white schools?

Mr. Powell: My mother was a half white woman and half Indian. My wife is in the Indian Territory.

Mr. Miller: How old are you, Mr. Powell?

Mr. Powell: Forty years.

Mr. Murphy: What is that fourteenth article?

Mr. Powell: The fourteenth article provides that all the Mississippi Choctaws or descendants of any Mississippi Choctaws whose ancestors had not moved to the Indian

Territory prior to June 28, 1898, should be admitted as Mississippi Choctaws, entitled to allotment, but this shall only apply under the rules of evidence, and shall not apply to any individual who is not a descendant of a Mississippi Choctaw.

Mr. Stephens: Now, I will present Mr. Nicholls. Mr. E. P. Hill: May I ask this witness a question j The Chairman: Yes; ask him one.

Mr. Hill: I want to identify him. Whereabouts in Oklahoma did you live?

Mr. Powell: At Homer. I had 2,500 acres there. They took it away from me, and then I went to Nowata.

Mr. Stephens: At Nowata? How do you spell it?

Mr. Powell: That is where my home was.

Mr. Hill: Nowata is in the Creek Nation?

Mr. Powell: No; in the Cherokee Nation. After I was knocked out of my land I secured a position in Old Mexico.

Mr. Hill: You were born in Mississippi?

Mr. Powell: Yes, sir. I was born 10 miles from where the treaty was made—Dancing Rabbit Creek.

Mr. Hill: Who carried you out to the Indian Territory?

Mr. Powell: L. P. Hutchinson. Mr. Hill: That was in what year? Mr. Powell: In 1902.

Mr. Hill: After you got there, did you locate in the town of Homer that you speak of?

Mr. Powell: Yes; near Ardmore.

Mr. Hill: And you lived there until 1907?

Mr. Powell: Yes, sir.

Mr. Stephens: He has a written statement.

The Chairman: Very well. That can be incorporated in the hearings.

34

WEST OF THE WATERS

THE FOLLOWING IS Alex's written statement referred to in the previous chapter by Congressional Speaker Stephens. Alex submitted this passionate statement, in his own words, along with his additional testimony given before U.S. Congress in 1910. It had become his mission to secure justice and mercy for disenfranchised mixed-race Indians like he and his family and to shed light on the crimes perpetrated against them.

To the honorable Committee on Indian Affairs:

36651—10 8 1 am the grandson of Tukeelublee on mv father's side, who was a full-blooded Choctaw Indian, and it was said by the older Indians he was at the treaty made between the United States Government and the Choctaw Indians September 27, 1830. I am the grandson o." Potubbee on my mother's side, and it was said by the older Indians that he was a child at the signing of the great treaty, when the Choctaws gave up all of their lands east of the Mississippi for the Indian Territory west of the Father of Waters, which was given to the Indian to rule and govern in his own way as long as the water runs and the grass grows. A supplemental treaty provides that all Mississippi Choctaws or their descendants who had not moved to the Indian Territory from Mississippi prior to June 10, 1896, should be considered Mississippi Choctaws, provided that where it appears of record that the applicant or ancestor through whom claim is made received the patent to lands in Mississippi or scrip in lieu thereof. In the year 1901 the Dawes Commission came to Mississippi for the purpose of identifying the Mississippi Choctaws that failed to go West when the other Choctaws emigrated from Mississippi to the Indian Territory. The Dawes Commission said to the Mississippi Choctaws, "You must go West to the Indian Territory and take up your land which you are entitled to under the fourteenth article of the treaty of 1830."

In obedience to the Dawes Commission, the Choctaws yielded to the wishes of the Dawes Commission, and they were shipped from Mississippi to the Indian Territory by speculators. When they landed in the Indian Territory, the native Choctaws claimed that the Mississippi Choctaws had no right to share in allotments of land in the Choctaw and Chickasaw nations on the ground that they failed to come West when the other Choctaws emigrated from Mississippi to the Indian Territory, and they therefore employed Mansfield, McMurray & Cornish, attorneys, of South McAlester, and paid them the sum of $750,000, with 10 per cent, and agreed to pay all their incidental expenses to turn the Mississippi Choctaws down. Mansfield, McMurray & Cornish had notaries public that they could control throughout the Choctaw and Chickasaw Nation. With these notaries public they could prove anything they wanted to prove.

For instance, if a Mississippi Choctaw had a case on

cause of action" for citizenship, in many instances they would send agents around and get up false affidavits from witnesses. I call your attention to my case. In February, 1904, I was advised by Copp & Luckett, attorneys, of Washington, D. C, if my grandfather Tukeelubbee moved to the Indian Territory shortly after the treaty of 1830 I would be entitled to be enrolled as an Indian of Choctaw blood. One Choc Franklin, of Homer, Ind. T., testified,>on oath, that on or about the year 1848 he came from Mississippi to the Indian Territory with Tukeelubbee and lived with him a greater part of the time up till his death, which occurred at Old Bougga Depot about the year 1869. One Bob Pettis, of Tatum, Ind. T., also one Bill Smith, of Tatum, Ind. T., knew Tukeelubbee after he emigrated from Mississippi to the Indian Territory up to the time of his death and were present at his burial, which occurred at Old Bougga Depot, in the Choctaw Nation, in the year 1869.

After establishing these facts of my grandfather, Tukeelubbee, I was further advised by Copp & Luckett, of Washington, D. C, to find some of the old rolls that bore Tukeelubbee s name in May, 1904. I was advised that one John M. Hodge, of Atoka, Ind. T., was in possession of the old rolls. I called on Mr. Hodge in regard to the old rolls. He advised me that the name of Tukeelubbee appeared on the rolls; that he had been in possession of several times. He also informed me that he had turned the old rolls over to Mansfield, McMurray & Cornish. I called on these three gentlemen in regard to the old rolls. They advised me that they were in possession of the old rolls, but would have to look them up. They claimed to have made a search for them but they failed to find them. They told me that they had turned them over to the Dawes Commission. I went to the

Dawes Commission and asked them if they were in possession of the old rolls.

They stated to me that the old rolls were in Washington, D. C. I failed to find any of the old rolls. The nation made assertion that neither my name nor my grandfather, Tukeelubbee, appeared on any of the old rolls. Mansfield, McMurray & Cornish notified my attorneys, Copp & Luckett, of Washington, D. C, that the name of Tukeelubbee did not appear on any of the rolls alter claiming to me that the old rolls were not in reach of them. On or about September 15, 1904, Mansfield, McMurray & Cornish sent two men in the neighborhood of Tatums, Ind. T., and Homer, Ind. T. These men were acting under the instructions of Mansfield, McMurray & Cornish. The names of these men were Moore and Fielding. They went to one Robert Pettis, one of my witnesses. Pettis could not read nor write. They claimed to Pettis that they were life-insurance agents. They asked him to sign papers, which he did. They told him in a few days he would receive his policy. They then made inquiry of Pettis about the Indians that came from Mississippi shortly after the treaty of 1830. Pettis became suspicious of these men and came to see me. They went to one Bill Smith and had him to sign papers as they did Pettis, claiming to be life-insurance agents. They went to Choc Franklin's home, the man who come from Mississippi with Tukelubbe. Franklin was not at home.

They claimed to Franklin's family that they were life insurance agents. They then went to one Edw. Carter, the notary public that took the affidavits of Franklin, Pettis, and Smith. They wanted to get affidavit from Mr. Carter; they tried to make him believe that they were after me for a debt. Carter discovered at once that these men were up to something wrong. Carter came to see me at once and I then notified my attorneys, Copp &

Luckett, of Washington, D. C. In a few days I received a copy of the affidavits from Washington, D. C, signed by Bob Pettis and Bill Smith, dated September 15, 1904, that they never knew any such man as Tukelubbe. I then got up counter affidavits and proved that Moore and Fielding went in disguise into the neighborhood of Tatum and Homer, Ind. T., claiming to be life-insurance agents. I then forwarded these affidavits to my attorneys in Washington,

1). C. This is the way hundreds of the Mississippi Choctaws have been treated, I ask the Committee on Indian Affairs of the Sixty-first Congress of the United States before winding up the affairs of the Five Civilized Tribes to make some legislation wherein the Mississippi Choctaws may receive their share of allotment of lands in the Choctaw Nation, Indian Territory, now Oklahoma, which is said to be the remainder of the once mighty tribe of red men. Their homes that once knew them east of the great Mississippi River will know them no more. Forever they are west of the Father of Waters, where they are fast disappearing.

Respectfully, yours,

A. P. Powell, Mississippi Choctaw Indian.

Mr. Balinger: He has the certificate here of his grandfather under article 14. If it is added it will make the record complete.

The Chairman: File it, and it will go with the record.
[Following is the certificate referred to:] Department of The Interior, General Land Office, Washington, D. C, March 14, 1910. I hereby certify that the annexed copy of Choctaw Certificate No. 272 B, is a true and literal exemplification from the original in this office.

In testimony whereof I have hereunto subscribed my name and caused the seal of this office to be affixed, at the city of Washington, on the day and year above written.

[seal.] H. W. Sanford,

Recorder of the General Land Office. No. 272 B.]

Certificate issued in pursuance of the provisions of the acts of 23d August, 1842, and 3d March, 1845, for one-half of claims under the fourteenth article of the treaty of September, 1830, made at Dancing Rabbit Creek, with the Choctaw Indians.

Whereas the commissioners appointed under the act approved on the 23d day of August, 1842, entitled "An act to provide for the satisfaction of claims arising under the fourteenth and nineteenth articles of the treaty of Dancing Rabbit Creek, concluded in September, one thousand eight hundred and thirty," have determined that Po tubbe, a child over 10 years of age, of Ok lah o man, a Choctaw head of a family, is entitled, under the fourteenth article of the treaty aforesaid, to a half section of land of 320 acres; and whereas the said determination has been concurred in by the Secretary of War; and whereas the United States have disposed of the land to which the said Po tubbe was entitled as aforesaid, so that it is now impossible to give the said child the quantity aforesaid according to the said article;

Now, therefore, pursuant to the acts approved the 23d August, 1842, and 3d March, 1845, this certificate is given by the Secretary of War, by direction of the President of the United States, that the said Po tubbe is entitled, if living, and if not, the heirs and legal representatives of the said child are entitled to 160 acres (being one-half of the above quantity) of land, to be taken out of any of the public lands in the States of Mississippi, Louisiana, Alabama, and Arkansas, subject to entry at private sale. Any assignment of this certificate must be attested by two credible witnesses. Given under the seal of the War Department this 6th day of October, 1845.

W. L. Marcy, Secretary of War.

T. Hartley Crawford, Commissioner of Indian Affairs. Po Tubbee (his X mark).

In presence of— John Drennen, Supt. Ind. Affrs. William Wilson.

I certify that the within names Po tubbee has voluntarily and in good faith transferred this certificate in my presence.

Rec: Vol. 4, P. 95. John Drennen, Pat. Dat. Jany 15/58. Supt. Ind. Affrs.

I, William O. Wilson, of Yell Co., State of Arkansas, assignee of Po tubbe do on this 19 day of July A. D. 1851, apply to locate the within Choctaw Certificate No. 272 B. on the southwest qr. of the northwest qr. Sec. No. eight & the northwest qr. of the southeast qr. & the south half of the southeast qr. in Section No. five, Township No. five No. of Range No. twenty West, containing 160 acres in full satisfaction of the same.

William Osem Wilson.

I hereby certify that the within Choctaw Certificate is located on the SW. i of the NW. } Sec. No. 8*& the NW. \ of the SE. J & the S. 4 of the SE. 1 in Sec. No. 5 Township No. 5 N of Range No. 20 W containing 160 as above applied for and agreeably to the acts under which it was issued.

John E. Manly, Register

35

THE COMMISSION
HAS THEIR SAY

THE COMMISSION SENT their top representatives for the Choctaw/Chickasaw E. P. Hill and George D. Rodgers, anticipating the testimony of this one man in particular, against whom they'd spent years fighting his constant requests for citizenship. Powell was now considered an enemy. The well-seasoned attorneys were armed to block any attempt within in these hallowed halls of justice to overturn the final ruling of the Dawes Commission against him.

Before discussing Alex's case specifically, the presiding Chairman and other legislators questioned the Indian Nations' lawyers on how it was determined whether or not a person was deemed of Indian ancestry. Alex was able to interject two questions of his own.

**Actual excerpts from the Congressional hearings on
April 2, 1910.**

The Chairman: Now, supposing the father was a full-blood

Choctaw and the mother had a trace of negro blood and only a trace. How about that case?

Mr. Rodgers: Well, if the mother and the children had been recognized by the tribe as Indian citizens, they would be enrolled as citizens, probably. The commission would not let that mere trace of negro blood serve to eliminate them from the tribal roll.

The Chairman: Did the tribe recognize or had the tribe, either by legislation or custom, at any time recognized any person of mixed negro and Indian blood as a citizen and so enrolled him

Mr. Rodgers: I mean to say that possibly there are some people of that class who are on the tribal roll, but from an examination of those rolls and an examination of the reputable men in the Choctaw and Chickasaw nation it was determined by the commission that it was the custom and usage of the tribes, as shown bv their laws and the way they consistently acted that the child should follow its mother, and that if the child had a negro mother it was not recognized as an Indian.

It gave them only certain blood.

Mr. Murphy: I will ask you if this is not a fact, Mr. Rodgers, that the Choctaws and Chickasaws always drew the line between the negro and the Indian, and the Creeks were so intermarried with the negroes that they did not know where to draw the line?

Mr. Rodgers: Yes. The Choctaws and Chickasaws, I think I can say without contradiction, were a race that always maintained a clear line between themselves and the negro, and had as much pride of race as the white people.

Mr. Murphy: And the Creeks did not?

Mr. Rodgers: No.

Mr. Saunders: That seems to have been fully developed here. Let me ask you: Suppose a Choctaw woman had an illegitimate child by a man descended from a Choctaw negro slave, what would be the tribal and property rights of that child (

Mr. Rodgers: A Choctaw Indian woman

Mr. Saunders: Suppose a Choctaw woman had an illegitimate child by a man descended from a Choctaw negro slave, what would be the tribal and property rights of that child?

Mr. Rodgers: I think the child would have followed the mother, undoubtedly, the Indian mother.

Mr. Saunders: Would there be any difference in a case such as this: Suppose, instead of being >i descendant of a Choctaw negro slave, a man had negro blood in him derived otherwise, that descendant, in that case, would still follow the Choctaw mother, would he?

Mr. Rodgers: Yes, sir; I think that is the general proposition.

Mr. Saunders: And if a Choctaw Indian had an illegitimate child by a woman descended from a Choctaw negro slave what would you say would be the tribal and property rights of that child?

Mr. Rodgers: They would be the same; it would follow the mother, I think.

Mr. Saunders: Mark you that such a woman, as suggested in that question, might have more Indian blood in her than negro blood, but would the strain of Indian blood in her cause that child to be denominated and classed as a negro? That has been stated here as a fact.

Mr. Rodgers: I think the commission would enroll her under this provision of section 21: It shall make a correct roll of all Choctaw freedmen entitled to citizenship under the treaties and laws of the Choctaw Nation, and all their descendants born to them since the date of the treaty.

Mr. Saunders: That would be a case of a full-blood Choctaw Indian who had an illegitimate child by a woman who may have been three-fourths Indian and one-fourth negro; in that case the child would be enrolled as a negro?

Mr. Rodgers: Yes; if the mother was a freedman I think the child would be a freedman too.

Mr. Saunders: The strain of Indian blood in the mother would not make the mother an Indian? If she had an eighth or a sixteenth, or something like that, she would still be classed as a negro?

Mr. Rodgers: That is the general rule in the tribe; yes, sir.

Mr. Saunders: That strain of negro blood would make her a negro?

Mr. Rodgers: Yes

Mr. Saunders: In the case of a Choctaw Indian who married a woman descended from a Choctaw negro slave there would be a legitimate union, and in that case the children would follow the mother, who had a strain of negro blood in her, however slight.

Mr. Rodgers: It would be a marriage that would be considered unlawful by the tribe, and as one to be frowned upon. If there were such cases they were certainly ostracized after their marriage. I think the child would take its status from its mother; I am satisfied that has been the general rule.

Now, there may be some very few exceptions; I cannot state that in every case they did that.

∽

Mr. Hinshaw: You think, Mr. Rodgers, there were no Choctaw citizens excluded from the rolls by the commission?

Mr. Rodgers: No Choctaw citizens?

Mr. Hinshaw: Yes.

Mr. Rodgers: These people who were entitled to enrollment and did not get on?

Mr. Hinshaw: Yes.

Mr. Rodgers: I won't say that. I will say the commission honestly and fairly passed on every scrap of evidence that was given before them. It might be, possibly, that some man who was entitled did not prove his case.

Mr. Hinshaw: You were there at the time mostly

Mr. Rodgers: Yes, sir.

Mr. Hinshaw: Acting for the commission?

Mr. Rodgers: Not acting for them; I was acting under them: I did not pass upon any cases myself, or anything like that.

Mr. Hinshaw: Well, I tried to get from Mr. McHarg the other day the modus operandi when an application came before the commission. What, in addition to the application, was insisted upon in each case to prove citizenship <

Mr. Kendall: Take Powell's application, for instance.
  he would have to prove that he was a descendant of" one of the Indians who went before the United States Indian agent in Mississippi within six months after the date of

the treaty of 1830 and signified ills intention of remaining in Mississippi.

Mr. Hinshaw: He would have to present witnesses to testify' to that fact, would he not?

Mr. Rodgers: Why, it would be impossible to have eyewitnesses; of course, if he could prove that he was a descendant, for instance, of a man named Iyakakubbe, or something like that, we would try to find that name on the list, and if he would prove conclusively

Mr. Hinshaw: Prove it, how?

Mr. Rodgers: Prove it by competent testimony; it would be by witnesses or by depositions. We had to adopt rules of testimony; you could not take ex parte affidavits from all over the country.

The Chairman: There would be rolls, would there not?

Mr. Rodgers: Yes, sir.

The Chairman: Were there rolls of the Mississippi Choctaws?

Mr. Rodgers. We had all the records which the commission could get hold of from the Indian Office or any place else relating to these Mississippi Choctaws.

Mr. Hinshaw: It has been alleged that in many cases a mere application was made, and upon that application citizenship was passed without further proof; is that correct?

Mr. Rodgers: Mere applications without anything to back them up?

Mr. Hinshaw: Yes.

Mr. Rodgers. Why, no; a man had to show his right. If a man came in and made application and the Indian commissioners said.it was all right—that they knew him—we would ask for his name and ask whether he was on the roll; get his name, and if his name was found on the roll, of course there was no need of any more evidence in that case.

Mr. Hinshaw: You took the word of the Indian commissioner who knew the man?

Mr. Rodgers: No, sir; his word and the rolls, if there was no objection from anybody.

Mr. Hinshaw: Well, then, the first step, upon an application being made, was to consult the roll, was it?

Mr. Rodgers: Yes, sir.

Mr. Hinshaw: Now, what roll?

Mr. Rodgers: Why, the rolls which were used by the commission, the roll of 1885, the foil of 1893, and the roll of 1896, with regard to the Choctaw Nation; and the rolls from the Chickasaw Nation were the rolls of 1878, 1893, and 1896.

Mr. Rodgers: In his case Choctaw;

Mr. Hinshaw: And if his name properly appeared on any of those rolls he was passed without question?

Mr. Rodgers: Yes, sir.

Mr. Latta: In other words, Mr. Rodgers, every Indian that applied to be put on the rolls, where there was no objection, was put on, was he not?

Mr. Rodgers: If he made prima facie showing and there was no objection; of course they required at least a prima facie showing.

Mr. Hinshaw: As a matter of fact, there was no testimony

actually taken in most of these cases, but mere consultation of the rolls?

Mr. Rodgers: Well, he was questioned; the applicant was questioned. In 1898 and 1899 the commission was right out in the Choctaw and Chickasaw nations, and the applicants were coming in there before them; they had the rolls with them; they questioned these applicants and they took down a memorandum and made cards, census cards. They took down sufficient information to identify the people, the names of the father and mother, the tribal enrollment of the person, where they lived, their post-office address, and so forth.

While it was not written out in the form of testimony, like this testimony will be, it was kept in the form of census cards, a record such as the United States Census Bureau has, giving a sort of history, in brief, of the family of the applicant.

Mr. Hinshaw: They would frequently come to cases which they would reject by reason of some irregularity, as, I suppose, that they were not upon some roll?

Mr. Rodgers: They were not rejected at once, but they would be put upon what was called a doubtful card, and they would, perhaps, take some testimony at the time in cases like that. The people would be told what was necessary and they could come in at any time before the commission and submit additional testimony showing their rights.

Mr. Hinshaw: What would be the reason for going upon this doubtful list?

Mr. Rodgers: Why, if persons insisted that they had tribal recognition in any way and were not found on the roll, or if their names were found on the rolls and the tribal officials said they had no right there, they were put upon the doubt-ful card, because further investigation was necessary.

Mr. Hinshaw: Would it occur sometimes that a name would be upon certain of these rolls and not upon certain others of them; that is to say, these rolls were supposed to be of the whole tribe, as I understand?

Mr. Rodgers: Yes, sir.

Mr. Hinshaw: Well, the roll of a prior year would contain the names and the roll of a subsequent year would not contain those particular names?

Mr. Rodgers: That might have happened; yes.

Mr. Hinshaw: Would that be sufficient to put applicants on the doubtful list?

Mr. Rodgers: Why, no. People, you know, may have been away when one roll was made up, but were on another roll; but in nearly every such case the people got on the roll, because the families generally listed them. I may have given a wrong impression about the rolls a moment ago, as I did not finish my statement. I told you that the captains... If the several counties prepared these rolls, made up lists; then they all met together and revised them; they looked them over and submitted them to the proper tribal authorities for approval. But the word of the captain alone was not taken; they were all headmen in these several counties and were familiar with all the people, and they could act justly.

Mr. Hinshaw: In the case of these people who are here complaining because of exclusion from the rolls, what was the chief difficulty with them in getting on? What was the objection the commission usually had to putting these people on who now seek admission?

Mr. Rodgers: In the freedmen class?

Mr. Hinshaw: No; I mean these people who have been excluded entirely from the Choctaw rolls.

∽

Mr. Powell: *May I ask a question?*

The Chairman: Yes.

Mr. Powell: *Do you believe when the Dawes Commission came to Mississippi that a Mississippi Choctaw, if he proved Indian blood through his father and his father was too young to comply with the fourteenth article, would have the right to prove that his grandfather complied, would he have the right to prove through his grandfather?*

Now, say, I claimed Indian blood through my father, and my father was too young to comply, would I have the right, then, to go and prove through my grandfather, would I or would I not?

Mr. Rodgers: I have no doubt if your father was so young at the time that he could not prove, himself, and his father did prove, why, probably your father got a quarter section under that treaty.

Mr. Powell: *Let me ask you another question? Would it be natural that the Dawes Commission would approve my position by my father being too young?*

Mr. Rodgers: Well, the committee has asked Mr. Wright to look those cases up.

Mr. Hinshaw: To what extent have the rolls made up by the commission been reviewed and modified by the federal courts, if you know?

Mr. Rodgers: Why, those are the only cases that I know of;

they were the cases which were stricken from the roll, or an attempt made to strike them from the roll within the last few days of the enrollment work, and it was held by the Supreme Court that the Secretary had no authority to do that and they were left on the roll.

Mr. Murphy: Have you personally examined the rolls, the tribal rolls of the Five Nations that are filed with the commission?

Mr. Rodgers: Many, many times.

Mr. Murphy: I will ask you if you remember examining carefully the rolls, the tribal rolls, of the Choctaws and Chickasaws?

Mr. Rodgers: Yes, sir.

Mr. Murphy: I will ask you if there is any mutilation in any of those rolls on file with the commission?

Mr. Rodgers: The rolls which were used by the commission, the rolls I have heretofore mentioned, the six rolls, I would say, are in excellent condition, and the Choctaw rolls of 1885 and 1893 are bound separately in counties, with permanent, substantial bindings, and I do not remember finding any mutilation of those rolls. I will say they are not mutilated.

The Chairman: Were those rolls in the possession of the commission, the rolls under the act of 1896?

Mr. Rodgers: Why, I understand that the 1893 and 1896 rolls were in the possession of the commission.

The Chairman: When did they get possession of the census roll of the Choctaw Nation of 1885?

Mr. Rodgers: They got possession of that in the latter part of 1902 or the first part of 1903, sometime about the 1st of January.

The Chairman: And they did not have that roll when they made the enrollment under the act of 1896?

Mr. Rodgers: Well, they did not make any rolls under the act of 1896.

The Chairman: What did they do?

Mr. Rodgers: The commission, under the act of 1896—and my time is pretty limited, and I want to go into that fully, because that is something which should be understood. In this work there is a distinction between the jurisdiction of the commission under the act of 1896 and the jurisdiction subsequent to that time. There was a commission established in 1893 that went down and made a report that there were certain fraudulent actions on the part of the tribes in removing people entitled to be enrolled.

Mr. Kendall: Ought not this to be taken up at another time? It is about time for adjournment.

Mr. Murphy: I have another question I would like to ask. Are there any writings of any character that you saw, such as cooking receipts, or things of that kind?

The Chairman: Or the elimination of names?

Mr. Latta: And erasures?

Mr. Rodgers: No, sir; the rolls that were used are in excellent shape. I will state in regard to that that the commission attempted to get everything that would look like a roll from these tribes. I know, because I went down to the capital at Tishomingo at one time and looked over all records in order to see if I could find anything. I did find some memorandum sheets just about that big [indicating], with a few names on them. Sometimes they were receipt books, with a few names in them, but they were never used as rolls. They are kept there in the vault, and anyone going down there to look over those things will find this mass of papers and find some papers that are mixed up with receipts; but the commission did not use them. They did not know what they were, but they went out and collected everything that looked like a roll.

Mr. Murphy: Is there any appearance on any of those Choctaw or Chickasaw rolls to show that pages have been cut out at any place?

Mr. Rodgers: No, sir; I do not think so.

(At 12 o'clock p.m. the committee adjourned to meet at 10 o'clock a. m. Tuesday, April 12, 1910.)

Before the legislators adjourned for the day, Alex had been led off of the Senate floor and into the hallway. From the outside steps, he looked up at the hallowed building where he was denied any further opportunity to address or question any of the Dawes attorneys' testimony. His mind then turned to Molly and the children and what news he would soon have for them.

Back home, Molly set out the last of the day's meal, but she herself could not touch it. She recalled their last conversation the night before Alex left for Washington.

"Baby, I believe in you, but I don't want you being consumed by this either…. Do you understand? I don't want you to lose hope, but I don't want that same hope to consume you, if it turns to desperation. Sometimes, I don't even know who you are anymore. I haven't been with you for weeks because you spend hours and days writing and planning your next strategy.

It has to end, and I hope and pray it does in Washington–for good–so we can get back to living our lives."

Alex was completely silent, and then said, "After all these years, I thought you understood."

Molly pursed her lips together and then whispered to her husband, "That's just it... it's because of so many years of watching and waiting, that I do understand what's happening to you. Never forget what I said... all I need is you and this family–nothing else."

36

PAST HAUNTS THE PRESENT

AS CONFUSION BEGINS to set in, Alex clings to his belief that God, family, and justice will prevail for he, Molly, and their now fifteen children. Meanwhile, Attorney J.W. Howell from the Office of the Assistant Attorney General of the U.S. Department of the Interior and other distinguished white men hold the life and future of the Powell family in their hands.

Actual Documentation of final Congressional hearing for Alex Phillips Powell

Washington, Monday, May 9, 1910.
The committee met this day at 10 o'clock a. m., Hon. Charles H. Burke, chairman, presiding.

The Chairman. The committee will come to order.

ADDITIONAL STATEMENT OF J. W. HOWELL,
ASSISTANT ATTORNEY,

OFFICE OF THE ASSISTANT ATTORNEY-GENERAL FOR THE INTERIOR DEPARTMENT.

The Chairman. They have appeared before the committee and have given their statements, and we want to know what the facts are in regard to them.

Mr. Howell: I will give you the case of A. P. Powell.

Mr. Person: There is an Anthony P. Powell and an Alexander P. Powell.

Mr. Howell: The record shows that A. P. Powell was an applicant for identification as a Mississippi Choctaw in 1901 at Meridian. Miss. At that time a field party, sent out by the Dawes Commission, visited certain points in Mississippi and took the testimony of persons who were applicants for enrollment. At that time Mr. Powell made statements by which he may be identified. That is to say, he gave the names of other members of his family besides himself. He has quite a large family.

The Chairman: Now, which Powell are you talking about? Does it appear whether his name is Anthony or Alexander?

Mr. Howell: The fact is that the records show almost conclusively that it is one and the same person.

Mr. Latta: The testimony you have shown that it is one and the same person? There are not two A. P. Powells?

Mr. Howell: I do not think there are two A. P. Powells. I think it is one and the same person.

The Chairman: Do you know whether or not there are

affidavits or other evidence filed to the effect that there are two Powells?

Mr. Howell: There were a number of affidavits filed, including the affidavit of this man himself, in 1904.

Mr. Ballinger: Mr. Chairman, if you will pardon me there, Powell was at my office this morning with the affidavit of one of the most prominent citizens of that country. I told him to give it to Mr. Howell and have him make it a part of that case. Evidently he has not seen Mr. Howell.

Mr. Howell: No. At any rate, in this testimony taken in 1904, he gave the names of the children of this large family, and he also gave the names of his parents, his ancestors, and the date of his birth, and things of that kind.

The Chairman: Have you the record of what was shown at that time?

Mr. Howell: Yes.

The Chairman: Will you give it?

Mr. Howell: I have not the record here, but in the original testimony the full name is given as "Anthony P. Powell," and after that in the correspondence it appears as "A. P. Powell " But this is the reason why I think they are one and the same: Some three or four years afterwards, I think in 1904, Copp & Luckett, a firm of lawyers of this city, filed a motion for a review, accompanying which was the affidavit of Mr. Powell, and in that affidavit he makes precisely the same statement in regard to the names of his children and of his mother's blood and his ancestry as was made in that original testimony that was taken in 1901. He thinks that there has been a mistake made, and he is justified in thinking so in regard to some minor matters. It seems that the stenographer who took the testimony has furnished Mr. Powell with a letter or affidavit in which he states that he thinks that he probably did make some mistakes, but he says he has never seen the testimony since it was transcribed, and he does not know, but he thinks he made some mistake about the parentage of this man. But, taking the record as a whole—I went through it very carefully and I spent three hours on it—it is my judgment that there is only one man in the case, and that A. P. Powell is the only person.

The Chairman: Now, the A. P. Powell that you are talking about at some time or other filed an application for review through his attorneys. Copp & Luckett'

Mr. Howell: Yes.

The Chairman: Of course, it ought to be a simple matter to show whether the A. P. Powell that is here is the man who filed the affidavit with Copp & Luckett.

Mr. Howell: This man claims to be a descendant of a Choctaw who was a resident of Mississippi in 1830, and that this ancestor complied with article 14 of the treaty of 1830, and the allegations and proof always run to this ancestor all the way through. This is the same ones that he relies on in conversation with me, so that it confirms that view* with quite a degree of certainty. His allegations were sufficient to warrant his enrollment as a Mississippi Choctaw had they been proved, but his proof was not sufficient to support his allegations, and while he made quite a strong showing in regard to Indian blood, he never removed to the Indian Territory until 1903, which is five years after the Curtis Act. His claim was adjudicated from two standpoints: First, as a Mississippi Choctaw, and he could not furnish satisfactory proof of his descent from these old Choctaws of 1830; and second, his claim by blood, which could not be allowed for two reasons: First, his name was not upon the tribal rolls, and second, he did not remove to the Choctaw Nation until

1903. Those are the facts such as I could get out of the case. I recollect that the ancestor through whom he claims on his father's side appears in the records of the Indian Office as a person who was two years old, I think, or three years old in 1830, and who was therefore born about 1827. To check up his statement, I notice that this A. P. Powell said that he himself was born in the year 1860. and he gave his father's age, and by calculation his father must have been born about two years after his alleged grandfather, and that would be on his father's side almost, conclusive proof that he was mistaken. But on his mother's side he also claimed descent from a Choctaw who complied with the treaty of 1830. I do not think there is any inconsistency there except just a lack of proof, apparently.

Mr. Hill: What did the proof show in that case?

Mr. Howell: His original statement is that his mother was part Indian.

Mr. Hill: I do not mean his statement. I mean what did the commission decide in regard to him?

Mr. Howell: I do not know what the decision held, apart from the evidence. It was a large record.

The Chairman: You have some papers from the department here bearing on the case?

Mr. Howell: I did not bring with me anything

The Chairman: Do they show the decision of the commission?

Mr. Howell: Yes; they contain that decision.

The Chairman: I notice that this man in his statement refers to a grandfather by the name of Tukelubbe. Is that the one you refer to?

Mr. Howell: Yes.

The Chairman: What do you say about him? He was born when?

Mr. Howell: According to the Indian Office the Tukelubbe who received scrip under the fourteenth article of the treaty of 1830, was born about the year 1827.

The Chairman: And this man himself claims to have been born in 1860?

Mr. Howell: Yes.

The Chairman: And he claims to be the grandson of this other man?

Mr. Howell: Yes; and he gave his own father's age. He said, if my recollection is right, and I know it is so far as the point is concerned, that his father died at the age of about 50 years; he says, along in 1878. At any rate the calculation was that his father must have been born about two years after Tukelubbe.

∽

Mr. Latta: Then there were only two- or three-years difference between the ages of his father and grandfather?

Mr. Howell: Yes; according to the record.

Mr. Latta: That is a mistake, of course.

Mr. Howell: But on his mother's side there is no apparent discrepancy, but only a lack of proof. Most of these people who sought identification as Mississippi Choctaws were too ignorant to establish proof. It was a long way off; the witnesses lived in Mississippi, and it was practically a physical impossibility to establish proof unless their cases were very good, unless they were full blood; and as a result there were only a very few mixed-blood Mississippi Choctaws identified.

Mr. Ballinger: In whose name, Mr. Howell, was the original application made?

Mr. Howell: In the stenographic notes it is "Anthony P. Powell."

Mr. Ballinger: This man claims to be Alexander P. Powell.

Mr. Howell: Yes. The records show his father to be Alexander Wilmer, and he claims to be Alexander, but whether it is Alexander or Anthony, all the papers in the case are consistent with the allegation that he is Anthony.

Mr. Ballinger: Is there not in the record there an affidavit of the stenographer who took the testimony, stating that he made a mistake in that name?

Mr. Howell: No. There is an affidavit or letter of the stenographer who took the testimony, saying that he thinks he might have made some mistake in connection with certain answers that were given, but he does not specify-the name of the applicant, and he is very vague, and he says, in substance, "I have not seen the testimony since it was transcribed."

The Chairman: Mr. Howell, in the files of the case are there any affidavits or application papers or other papers purporting to have been signed by this man Powell?

Mr. Howell: Yes; there are numerous papers.

The Chairman: Then I wish you would furnish the committee with some of those papers in order that the committee may compare them with the signature that this man makes at the present time.

Mr. Howell: Yes. I compared those signatures, and while I thought they were the same, they were not of such uniformity as satisfied my mind that they were the same. But the contents were what governed me in my conclusion.

Mr. Latta: Does the records that you have shown in any place that there were two A. P. Powells?

Mr. Howell: No; there is nothing to show that. The post office is always the same, and all the correspondence goes to A. P. Powell.

Mr. Latta: And the names of the children of A. P'. Powell and Anthony Powell are the same?

Mr. Howell: Yes; and there are about thirteen of them, and their names are such that there could be no mistake about it.

Mr. Ballinger: Mr. Howell, I would like to ask one question further. In the testimony offered by the nation I think there were some affidavits filed in that case by the nation opposing the enrollment of this man. Does it not appear in that testimony that the witnesses were talking about Anthony P. Powell and not about Alexander P. Powell?

Mr. Howell: I do not remember that testimony well enough to make an exact statement on that point. I would not like to make a statement about that...

⸙

Mr. Kendall: Have you examined the records fully in the case of A. P. Powell? Have you?

Mr. Rodgers: Yes, sir; I went through that record fully.

Mr. Kendall: From your examination of the record, have you any doubt that a mistake was made as to the identity}' of that man?

Mr. Rodgers: Two names appear in that record; one Alexander Powell, and the other Anthony Powell. That is the only Mississippi Choctaw Powell case that can be found in the records of the commission or the department, and I have no doubt in my own mind but that

The Chairman: I will say, Mr. Kendall, that there is a communication here from the department giving considerable in the way of details in the Powell case, and it discloses a rather remarkable condition of affairs if there are two Powells.

Mr. Kendall: If there are two?

The Chairman: Yes; if there are two. They each had the same number of children, and each had the same name and were of the same age, and with the same grandfather and same father. It is a little strange if there are two individuals with that condition existing.

Alex had left the final day of the proceedings with a sense of foreboding. It would have taken him two weeks to get home after giving his statement, but he believed he should spend all his time contacting more upstanding citizens who were acquainted with him and his efforts. He hoped if he could acquire the testimony of this one last gentlemen, then Congress would force the Commission to do right, and he could return to Molly with his pride intact, as a leader of his people—someone she could respect.

He had finally acquired the affidavit of one of the most prominent citizens in the country, Eugene Debs, who Alex conferred with when he traveled from Mississippi to Oklahoma. Alex was inwardly incensed when the clerk denied him the opportunity to present the document, after initially being told by one of the presiding officials that he could, only days earlier.

Alex's mind wavered between hope and fear with one final

plea to the honorable legislators… one which he would never be allowed to utter inside on the Congressional floor.

"Do you understand how hard it is for a man to watch his family suffer?–THIS MAN—because I am a man like you! I cannot sleep or eat anymore because I won't live this way! Like so many men of the South, do you also believe that I don't have a mind or soul? That I'm somehow different… not the same… made lesser? Won't you see me as a man—also made in God's image, who deserves the same rights and privileges of humanity!?

Pulling out his starched handkerchief, Alex held it to his face and groaned audibly, trying to keep fear from overcoming his tiny ray of hope.

"Lord… lord… please have mercy!" he moaned quietly. "I know I'm not perfect, but if there is any humanity in anyone here, please… please have them do right by your creation, so I can do what is right by Molly and my children as you, my God, would have any man–WHICH I AM–to do."

Just as he had entered, Alex exited through the tall glass doors and descended the long, imposing stairway, then deliberately paced his steps back to his tiny room at the hotel. This time the magnificence of the Capitol building, its expansive green lawns, beautiful trees and artwork were invisible to him for a different reason–only the court's decision to be rendered in a few hours mattered.

Alex had waited to be notified before he left Washington of their decision. The men who had taken an oath, who swore to protect his rights as a human being had failed him. This was his ultimate attempt for justice—a final time to have his say. What had he said wrong? Did they have more questions of him? Why didn't they call him back in and allow the new affidavit? He could have explained anything… anything if someone had more questions. Did they reject the other man who came with him, he wondered—losing focus. He had been forced to leave his home in Mississippi… gone to Indian Territory in Oklahoma… now traveled to Washington because he believed once here—honorable men would uphold his rights and be an answer to his prayers.

He wondered if following the protocols set before him had allowed one or two attorneys representing the Indian Commission to persuade the congressmen to uphold their original judgement. Now he wondered if someone had been following him when he left the Capitol. He could have sworn that someone was trailing him.

From nowhere, he relived the day he allowed the census man to write down what he wanted—because the law gave them that right. How he did get the stenographer in Meridian to admit that some of the transcripts were incorrect. Was that done on purpose? Did those census takers carelessly write what they pleased, because they knew it wouldn't be challenged?

Now talking aloud to himself, Alex's mind grappled for answers, "That attorney who spoke before me, Mr. Cantwell, tried. He spoke the truth, but the others must have been too powerful for him. Was this their decisive action? Their plan to remove this thorn in their side—so determined to bring me down?"

Alex recalled the short conversation he had with Cantwell when the man first entered the Capitol building. Alex and the other man had been waiting out in the hall a long while to enter the congressional floor.

"I'm not here just for myself–my family and me." Alex told him.

"I understand." Cantwell nodded.

"You see, I was able to get more education than the others, so someone has to get help for them, too." Alex, said, "I talked to ten families before I was forced to leave Mississippi in '02 and they know of others like us who had the same thing done to them."

Cantwell began, "These last ten years, I've seen more... ," but, his words cut off in mid-sentence as he was summoned into the chambers to speak ahead of the other men.

Although the short interaction was all Alex had with Cantwell, after overhearing some of his testimony through the partially closed doors, Alex had thanked the Lord for this man whom he had been sure was also an answer to prayer.

37

RECOGNITION
WITHOUT REWARD

AROUND THE TIME Alex left home in April 1910, the census man showed up on the Powell's doorstep, as he did every 10 years since Molly could remember. Since Molly's husband was still head of the household, she insisted the annoying stranger put down her husband's information, as if he were here in the room with them. Molly had prayed all night, hoping this act of confidence on her part, would be a positive sign to God that she still believed in Him, and he'd soon bring her man home safely. But it was not to be.

On the 1910 recorded census the enumerator put her down as Mary once again, Alex down as A.P instead of Anthony P. this time (Alexander Phillips, perhaps?). However, every one of their children's names were listed correctly. The enumerator began with Alex as *Powell, A.P.*, at the sixth row down on the top section of the page. There were two sections on the page of the man's bulky, black leger to be completed. A top section and a bottom one. On the bottom part, every single member of the Powell family were all listed as *Choctaw Indians*, yet not one of them received any of the land rights that went with that label. Nothing.

With thirteen children still in the house, the family took up almost the entire page, using the last 15 slots at the top half and bottom half of the page. The official name on the record was the *THIRTEENTH CENSUS OF THE UNITED STATES: 1910 INDIAN POPULATION* recorded in Graham Township, Carter County, Oklahoma. Molly wondered if her family would ever be recognized as anything more than Indian in name only, and considered worthy to be added to the Choctaw Indian Rolls.

1910 Federal Census, Carter County, Oklahoma

PART VII

38

SHEDDING LIGHT

I T WAS ON the 20th day of May that Alex's attorney's Mr. Yancy and Mr. Lee first came to the house to deliver the decision Congress came to on Alex' case. Mr. Yancy said the legislative committee had one fair-minded member who was in support of granting "your husband" all that he has been fighting for all these years; however, the other three, especially one of them, convinced the others that Alex was too polished and not worthy of them overturning the Commission's decision. The attorney added that although their report stated otherwise, rumor is that their chief reason for denying Alex all that was rightfully his was that they believed that he may not have been who he said he was.

"I'm sorry Mrs. Powell." Mr. Lee added, "We know the herculean efforts your husband has put forth all these years–the appeals, evidence and scores of affidavits—but it still wouldn't prompt them to reverse the Commission's decision."

Though Molly had been completely devastated with the

decision in Washington, she was grateful for the attorneys' understanding. But the worst feeling was that none of it explained where Alex was at that moment. When the men left, Molly had been undecided whether or not to share what she was just told with the younger children, although her eldest daughter felt she should.

Molly believed Alex's not coming back right away had everything to do with the ruling. He was expecting so much from those men in Washington. He was so sure they would be different. She realized it could have taken almost two weeks just to get home, but it had been over two months and no word. Now that she'd learned of the decision, she prayed that it would eventually spark some desire to seek comfort in the arms of his family and lead him back to her and the children.

"I don't know what to do, Sista," Molly cried out, feeling the need to be even closer to her eldest daughter, calling her by her nickname. "I know he loves us with everything that's in him. He's probably somewhere still fighting… 'trying to be a good husband and father and save us from the life they've pressed us into,' is how he put it."

≫

Four months had passed since Alex had gone. Then in that same year, an August 1910 newspaper headlines publicized new revelations about the Commission, "***Vice-President Involved in Indian Scandal*** ."

Molly expressed little interest.

What does that matter to me now—to us … how much men cheat and steal? All she cared about… what she wanted was her husband back. Nothing else.

≫

Molly sat at the kitchen table peeling potatoes. As the skins fell onto the table to be separated, she couldn't separate her mind from reality.

I know I wasn't as supportive as I should have been just before you left, but you wouldn't leave me here alone with the children, no matter how hard it got... would you? Could you really desert me and the children—never come back... no I won't believe it! It's got to be something's holding you back... what more could they do to you?!

"They just squashed him like a grasshopper." Molly groaned audibly, releasing all the pain she believed her husband must be somewhere feeling—shaking her head and wringing her hands.

Eveline walked in the room to see her mother moaning and sobbing.

"Mother dear... mother?" Eveline couldn't hold back her own tears, watching her mother's pour from her eyes.

"I'm alright, Sista."

Recalling her own mother's strength, Molly wiped her face with the edge of her yellow and blue, daisy- trimmed apron, tied securely around her waist.

"I'll be fine, and I want you to be happy. That's what I want for you–a life of your own choosing. You deserve it. Everything you've been through with your father and me. You know he wanted you to have that chance to go to one of those teacher's colleges up North. I visited there years and years ago... propped right in the center of Boston it was. He would've been happy too, if you decided to go and marry," Molly added, "Although that would have been his second choice for you–after the teacher's college."

"Mother," Eveline cried. "I couldn't go anywhere now that I see you need me, I've changed my mind."

"No! My sweet girl. Go! Get away from here. You have to go! There's no future here, not like the one you could have. You will get your chance now. You either get yourself into a teacher's college or marry a good man or else!"

Eveline smiled, wrapping her arms around her mother's sturdy waist and placing her head on her mother's shoulder.

"And you know what mother?" She pulled away and stared into her mother's tired, glassy eyes, "Maybe father will be back home one day soon, before I either get married or go away to a teacher's college."

"You know… you're right. He maybe… will at that. I'm gonna hold on to that thought. She said, cupping her daughter's face in both hands, "He will be home one day… you and I both know it! Now let's start making plans for you. I won't have my oldest daughter looking like a pauper wherever she's going."

Molly kissed her stalwart child on both cheeks and held onto her hand. So relieved, Eveline would soon be on her way to the kind of life that she wanted for her. "Sista," had just the right amount of her mother's spunk and spirit that she'd be fine wherever she decided to go. Sista could have left long before now if all her time wasn't spent watching after her brothers and sisters and helping take care of the family all these years, Molly thought. The young men, even before we left Misterton, made it no secret that they would have liked to become her suitor, but she didn't want to be left behind in Misterton while her mother, father and siblings were being forced off their land and out of their home.

Determined not to focus on life as it was during that period, Molly reached further back to the days of her own youth, when she had been a mere slip of a girl, on her way to her own adventure, leaving Grenada County and the South behind…

Molly remembered approaching Milcreek Pond in a shiny black carriage. She was positive that the trees had been there forever, just waiting for this day to arrive. Ma and Alex would be there to share the moment with her. She had hoped others would come and help lead the way to the future—moving everything forward. Everything woven together in the tapestry of time. She could not separate anything, nor would she ever try. All were a part of her—the good times and the bad; connected and cared for, watched over, always by the Creator of time itself.

Another week passed. Molly was back to telling herself again.

One day at a time, he'll be back. He's safe. We've been through too much together for him to be gone for good. Nothing… , he said when he left, would ever take him away from me and the children. My husband will be back before year end. He may still write me if he doesn't have money left for a telegram. Yes, he will.

"I'll go to the post again next week—a letter may be there," Molly told Sista, who quietly mourned her mother's resurgence of hopefulness. Sista didn't tell her mother that she too had checked at the postmaster the week before.

"Yes," Molly said bravely, squeezing her daughter's hand. "I'll give it one year."

39

A LONG WAYS GONE

MAYBE IT WAS the severe snowstorms making its way across central and southern Oklahoma that year. The blizzard conditions, with heavy sleet and snow, moving across the Great Plains with 60 mph wind gusts, drove home the reality, that after four years of hoping Alex wasn't coming home.

Molly finally rested in the realization that not only would her family have to plan for life without her husband and their father, but also something sinister must have happened to him to prevent his return. Had it been eleven years ago that they had packed up all the children to come here to Oklahoma? Now she alone. She prayed the United States would stay out of the war over in Europe, and she wouldn't have to prepare for her sons to be whisked across the ocean to battle. She needed to be strong for all their sakes.

⥲

For a year now, Sista had been corresponding by mail with a widower from Lonoke County, Arkansas. He came to visit his youngest children in Homer (Carter County). They were sent there to live with relatives after his wife died. When Molly asked how in the world they met, Eveline assured her mother she hadn't answered any advertisement in the *Carter Express* or *Star Gazette* from men in search of a wife.

"Sista, you know you don't have to marry him," Molly told her.

"I know mother, but I'm past 25 and we don't have the space we had back home in Grenada. After we're married, I will send money if I can."

"I wish your father could have met him."

"Of course, you'll meet him before we marry, mother, and so will everyone. We plan to make our home in Arkansas," Eveline happily shared. And he's written me some beautiful letters and writings. Did I tell you he is a teacher *and* a cotton farmer? I think I will be well taken care of, and will do my best to be a good wife to him, and take care of his little motherless children."

Molly felt both pride and sadness as she witnessed her confident daughter's transition to a new life.

"I've always felt so loved by you and Father," Eveline said fondly. "I know he did everything in his power for us and would have come back if he could.

"I remember you once told me Grandma, your Ma said, 'We all have something, a seed, deep inside of us, when we come into this world.' Her words helped me appreciate the hardships you, father and all of us have struggled through. I believe this world wants to purge that seed from people like us. But we won't let them, will we?"

Molly scooped up her sewing, and laid it down again, then crossed the space of vulnerability to be near her daughter's deep thoughts that sounded so much like her own—once.

"It's how we keep going, doing what we're special at; like you at sewing. No one had to teach you. Even talking. Some people naturally talk constantly about interesting things, and others learn from them.

"Sometimes, though, I think folks who talk all the time

don't want to think; maybe it hurts them to think. Maybe when they stop talking, all the painful thoughts rush into their heads."

Molly joined in, "My brother, your uncle, was a quiet person, always writing things down. I was the one who rattled on all the time. He would pretend to listen for only so long and find something else to do. Our Ma listened to me though, until I was finished, and when I started up again, too. She never talked for long. Maybe Ma didn't want to. I always believed she had pushed bad things out of her mind to make room for my constant prattle. It helped her keep going."

Eveline touched her mother's arm, anticipating more revelations, and then changed courses when none came.

"Why do you think they didn't rule in Father's favor, Mother?"

Molly sighed. "I can't say for sure, but I know it wasn't just. But if they had done right by your father, he would've been back home to us long ago. I remember before his attorney came by, I went to all the neighbors and asked if they had heard anything, and then sent a telegram to Washington, D.C., asking if Alex had been then there and left. It was confirmed. Alex had been in Washington at least that was something they could tell me."

Molly rose up and reached for her sewing shears to finish cutting out a pattern design for Eveline's walking suit she would wear on the long train ride to Arkansas next year. The ensemble was a long slim skirt, neatly fitted blouse and lightly fitted jacket.

"I believe God has something better for us," Molly decided, "but sometimes it takes from one generation to the next—like it did with Abraham."

40

A MAN SUCH AS THIS

SOME SAY ALEX went mad after he learned that his last attempt at justice had failed. When he learned of the court's decision on May 10, his only thought was of Molly and his children. He had no way of knowing how one enumerator's mistake, years ago, would come back to haunt him and give the government an excuse to question his credibility.

Alex, a strong man, tried to hold back a wall of tears. When he stepped outside, he used the back of his hand to fend off the glare of the sun. For so many years, he had given his all. And with their pronouncement, a body of comfortable men with authority and power dismissed his fight, sealed his fate and erased his hope.

∽

The mysterious stranger, a distinguished gentleman with faded emerald-gray eyes and a broken spirit, told doctors and hospital staff that his title was Government Agent. They even called him, "Chief." No one suspected that this mysterious man was the missing link to someone's life—an entire families'. That he had been a warrior.

As the man named Alexander Phillips Powell lay in a hospital bed, his last breaths were slow, and death was close. Molly and the children would never know about his ending, and neither would others who lived then, and who loved Alex.

His death certificate, dated 1917, was found 80 years later by his grandson. It showed that his last three years of life had been spent in Houston, Texas, 68 Dallas Street, where Alex finally passed away.

So many questions still remain. One was how Alex ended up in Texas? Was he prospecting for land that was free for the asking there? Had he become mentally crippled by years of failure and rejection and too ashamed to return home to Molly and the children without a land deed? Nothing.

According to other documents discovered many years later, some speculate that Alex had acquired a good amount of land in Houston that was later acquired by a hotel chain when he mysteriously died, according to his death certificate, from an asthma attack.

Others wonder, did the "insurance investigators" track him and finally decide that he'd caused them enough trouble?

Or, did he ultimately experience a devastating emotional wound? Not much different from that of his cousin Cioak. Both men so drained by those who continued to deny their lifelong existence, that their hearts and minds could no longer bear the strain.

In the end, Alex had taken on the identities of his oppressors, calling himself *Chief Alexander Powell, Government Agent.* The doctor called him that too and listed the title on his death certificate. Alex had prayed to God every day, and *He* knew his real name; and how the man called Alex shrunk, after he testified one last time in Washington, D.C.

Among his neighbors, you could still hear furtive whispers, "What happened to him? Wasn't he the so-called highfalutin one who was educated with the whites? He had been a leader to his people, fighting to support his family and neighbors, as a father, husband and friend. A good man he was."

Hopefully, those who would crush such a man's spirit without reason, and kill his family's hopes and dreams, will one day have to answer to a higher judge.

41
MOLLY'S RESOLVE

THE NEXT YEAR came, bringing with it Eveline's approaching marriage. Alex still hadn't returned home. Everyone suspected he wouldn't, but no one could say it. Molly hoped no one heard her wailing in her bed the night before. She did her best to muffle her cries with her pillow. It was another dream, but this time she was able to touch him, and they held on to each other for dear life. Molly knew she had to make a decision within herself, to be stronger. She had done it before.

But this time, she said to herself, "Got to be stronger, not just when everyone can see, but for me."

With the possibility of three of her boys heading off to war, she offered up a vow and a request to God and those she loved. "I will take this portion I've been given, and with your help, make the very best life for me and the children, as I am able. I have no time to show my sorrow where others can see or feel the misery I have in my heart." Feeling her own mortality, Molly also called on God for strength for her journey: "Since I only have so much time left to keep living, I will need a dose of that joy; the one Ma taught me all about."

After conversing with her Maker—fighting to be more than a shadow of her former self, Molly called all the children into the room and proclaimed, "I may still be on the sunny side of fifty, but who would want a widow woman with you wild, beautiful children. So, if I can't find someone who will love and take care of us like your father did, then I don't need anyone else. All I need is my wild bunch, right here."

Molly's entire brood gathered around their mother, laughing and hugging. This was the best time they had together in a long while.

≈§

More than ten years passed. Almost all the children were now grown, and Molly had kept her vow. Then, one November morning in the year 1927, she traveled to Colorado to visit her youngest daughters. While there, Molly's dreams and vision of the life she was born to live swirled about her. It included Ma, and of course, Alex smiling, and the children sitting next to him. They all were together beside the little lake that Molly loved so dearly at her childhood home.

She slowly fell to her knees, clasping her hands together. She whispered a prayer of thanksgiving for her children and the youthful days she lived at Milcreek Pond. "Lord, I will never forget… and will carry all my sweet loves in my heart for the rest of my days. One day our children, even our children's children, will come together to fulfill your promise."

There it was. Again before her. Molly returned to the unforgettable oasis where she and Alex first met.

With a life of its own, the lake approached as she strolled through the avenue of trees, swiveling on her heels to transfix her eyes to the full glorious sight. The tranquil waters reflected brilliant shades of blue, echoing the early morning sky. Willows and spruce on the other end of the pond mirrored on the surface of the water, as leaves rustled, revealing

the colors of autumn. Alex was there to meet her with the
child she'd lost, and Ma.

Outside the ground was damp, but the sky was clear and
summer blue, deeper than it had ever been in the mountains of
La Junta. Inside, a brilliance surrounded Molly, giving warmth,
joy and lasting peace. Now, it was hers to embrace forever.

Epilogue

Dear Great-Grandfather Alex,

Your life and struggle were not in vain. It took 100 years to find the truth and I pray as you did, so many times, so long ago that in the end you finally found peace. You fought the good fight and never gave up. Some may say you lost, but the legacy you've passed down from generation to generation is one of courage and perseverance in the face of insurmountable obstacles. The unsympathetic and oppressive system you endured was not yours to end, but you had hope that it would indeed end one day. You would be proud to know that your life's efforts were fruitful and sustaining. Your children, grandchildren, great children and others have pressed forward and will continue to pass on yours and Great-Grandmother Molly's legacy to future generations.

Love, Kay

Alexander Phillips Powell

References in Alphabetical Order:

Ancestry.com. U.S., Native American Applications for Enrollment in Five Civilized Tribes, 1898-1914 [database on- line]. Provo, UT, USA: Ancestry.com Operations, Inc., 2013. Original data: Applications for Enrollment of the Commission to the Five Civilized Tribes, 1898–1914. Microfilm M1301, 468 rolls. NAI: 617283. Records of the Bureau of Indian Affairs, Record Group 75. The National Archives at Washington, D.C.

AFL-CIO, Key People in Labor History, Eugene V. Debs https://aflcio.org/about/history/labor-history-people/eugene-debs

Brief and Argument of Harry J. Cantwell (of Crews & Cantwell, Attorneys-at-law, St. Louis, Mo.) Dec. 3, 2009, Library of Congress (https://www.loc.gov/item/10025856/)

(A) Contested Presence: Free Blacks in Antebellum Mississippi, 1820–1860: http://www.mshistorynow.mdah.ms.gov/articles/45/a-

Encyclopedia of Mississippi History Vol. 2: https://bit.ly/2Y7GrsN

Historical and Biographical Memoirs of Mississippi... Most Worthy and Illustrious Families/Individuals 1892, p.p. 91

Hochschild JL, Powell BM. Racial Reorganization and the United States Census 1850-1930: Mulattoes, Half-Breed

Mixed Parentage, Hindoos, and the Mexican Race. Studies in American Political Development. 2008;22 (1) :59-96.

Major events of late 1800's https://www.thoughtco.com/timeline-from-1880-to-1890-1774041

Mulatto Classification of Indian Families & Related Laws, By Stacey Ricketts, 10 Sep 2006 https://bit.ly/2U352zK

Native Americans National Archive https://www.archives.gov/research/native-americans/dawes/dawes-1896.html

National Register of Historic Places https://npgallery.nps.gov/GetAsset/2c80965a-094d-4b92-838c-feff5cb39651

Oklahoma Climatological Survey http://climate.ok.gov/summaries/monthly/2007/MCS_Febr uary_2007.pdf

Oklahoma Historical Society –The Dawes Commission https://www.okhistory.org/publications/enc/entry.php?entry =DA018

Sue Kidwell, "Allotment," The Encyclopedia of Oklahoma History and Culture, www.okhistory.org http://www.okhistory.org/publications/enc/entry.php?entry=AL011

Techniques of Direction Disenfranchisement-Success of the disfranchisement of black votes in the August 1900 election http://umich.edu/~lawrace/disenfranchise1.htm

Timetoast timelines- Native American Timeline from 1800- 1900 https://www.timetoast.com/timelines/native-american-timeline-1800-1900

United States. Congress. House. Committee on Indian Affairs, Choctaw And Chickasaw Rolls: Hearings Before the Committee On Indian Affairs, House Of Representatives, Seventy-first Congress, Second Session, On… 19552 And H.r. 22830 [March 18-May 13, 1910] by United States. Congress.

House. Committee on Indian Affairs. Pp.81- 116 https://en.wikipedia.org/wiki/Dawes_Commission

ABOUT THE AUTHOR

Kay Carroll leads a busy life teaching high school students about U.S. History and the relevance of their own lives and backgrounds. She lives with her husband in Northern Illinois.

Please Share your Opinion

ALEX'S EYES

https://www.amazon.com/review/create-review/error?ie=UTF8&channel=awUDPv3&asin=1723499552

MILCReeK PoND

https://www.amazon.com/review/create-review/error?ie=UTF8&channel=awUDPv3&asin=1478246502

InDigo Sky

https://www.amazon.com/review/create-review/error?ie=UTF8&channel=awUDPv3&asin=1534736190

Made in the USA
Monee, IL
08 March 2023

29422748R00141